CENSORSHIP
IN
AMERICA

by Olga G. and Edwin P. Hoyt

CENSORSHIP
IN
AMERICA

DISCARD

THE SEABURY PRESS • *NEW YORK*

Contents

CHAPTER 1

Censorship?

A SLIM young man sat in a narrow store, so narrow—only a door's width—that when two people entered what was really a corridor the shop was crowded. On the walls hung Zodiac cards, and on the shelves were books on astrology, witchcraft, and off-beat cooking. It was clearly a place appealing to those interested in the occult. The name of the store was The Hierophant; it was located on Main Street of historic Annapolis, near the old Market Place and the city docks where the oyster boats lay side by side.

The young man was the owner. At 5:30 p.m. one day in November, 1969, he was arrested on charges of selling pornographic materials, and taken to jail. The material confiscated included copies of an underground newspaper called *Yellow Dog*, five copies of the *Evergreen Review*, *The Collected Drawings of Aubrey Beardsley*, three copies of assorted underground comics, Yoga meditation books, selections from Oscar Wilde, and John Bunyan's *Pilgrim's Progress*.

A week before the arrest similar material had been

bought at the store by the police and taken to the state's attorney's office for an opinion. A judge who also viewed the material and the state's attorney's office concurred that the literature was in violation of obscenity laws, and a warrant for search and seizure was then issued. The Deputy Chief of Police of Annapolis said later, "I've seen stuff with so-called redeeming social value but this was really bad." He also admitted that there was no evidence of sale to minors, but "I'll tell you one thing, though: If any parents went into that store, they'd be on our necks in a minute."

The owner of The Hierophant, an attractive, clean-shaven young man, had a different view about the material he was selling. He insisted that it was not pornographic and said that he had seen the officer who purchased the material alleged to be "lewd, obscene, and indecent" on the premises many times in the weeks prior to the arrest. Indeed, on one occasion he had thrown the officer out of the store after he asked specifically for "dirty books."

The usual clientele, the owner said, were intellectuals. Many housewives and college professors frequented his establishment, while children did not. A sign was posted near certain materials forbidding them to minors.

In discussing the case after he was released on bail and back in his little cramped store, the owner was thoughtful. "I feel," he said, "that they objected to material that they felt was anti-religious. They had to hang something on me, so they hung the pornography." He had now decided to show all his material to the city officials first before displaying it, for approval or disapproval. "I can't stay in business, if I keep getting arrested." He could not afford to fight.

Less than two months later the lock was back on the door of The Hierophant, and the light inside no longer burned.

Did this case reflect censorship?

Censorship is a word derived from the Latin, and also a concept based on the Roman idea of social and legal justice. The word "censor" comes from the Latin *censere*, which means to tax, to value, or to judge, or all three. A censor in ancient Rome was one of the magistrates acting as census takers, assessors, and inspectors of morals and conduct. If a citizen failed to maintain a standard of civic duty, a *nota censoria* was placed on the rolls opposite his name.

Today, the meaning given to the term "censorship" varies from the very specific to the very broad. Psychoanalytically speaking, the censor is the psychic agency that represses unacceptable notions before they reach consciousness. In the wider social sense, however, censorship generally refers to official prohibition or restriction of any type of expression believed to threaten the established order.

There are many kinds of public censorship. There is political censorship, invoked by local and/or national government to keep itself in power. There is military censorship, invoked for the protection of the nation on a far more specific basis—the prevention of assistance to an enemy. There is religious censorship, such as the control of reading material that might tend to undermine the faith of the faithful, as adjudged by the church authorities. There is the censorship of the teacher who takes a comic book from a student, and of the neighbor who raises her eyebrows at a miniskirt. There is overt and subtle censorship; preventative and punitive, according to whether it is exercised before or after the objectionable expression has been made public. There are many kinds of censorship, for in the aggregate there are many forces attempting in numerous ways to supervise our political, social, and moral behavior.

Of all these kinds, perhaps the most controversial in the history of the United States has been that of cultural censor-

ship—censorship of the written word, of movies, the theater, art, radio, and television. In this book, we shall undertake to deal with those forces that have attempted to
supervise the cultural life of this country. We shall concen-
trate on the central question to be asked of any such attempt at cultural censorship, whether past or present: Who
is to be the judge of the public morals? Which of us is so
superior to his fellows in taste and morality that he can tell
us what to read, what to see, what to experience—what to
think?

CHAPTER 2

Early Censorship of the Written Word

W E I N America often think of censorship in terms of the Puritans and their stern way of living, but actually the concept of censorship is ages old, and not restricted to what we call Western civilization.

A famous ruler in China, Tsin Chi Hwangti, who built the Great Wall, was one of the first known men to try to control what people read. In 213 B.C. he declared that all "literature" was forbidden, with the exception of books that concerned science, medicine, and agriculture. All other books he ordered burned.

Throughout history there have been many other examples of those who sought to control the written word. Julius Caesar conducted an extensive book burning during his siege of Alexandria from 48 to 47 B.C. At that time this library contained probably the greatest collection in the world, and the loss of its carefully collected materials was no less than catastrophic.

The destruction of the Alexandria library did not end with Caesar. According to some sources, over the years more than 700,000 rolls of manuscripts were burned in one attack after another by Christians, Romans, and finally the Arabs who conquered Alexandria in 642. The Arab leader Omar even used books to heat the baths, seemingly with no regrets for his action. "These books," he said, "are either in accordance with the teaching of the Koran or they are opposed to it. If in accord, then they are useless, since the Koran itself is sufficient, and if in opposition, they are pernicious and must be destroyed."

This early censorship of books was not based on censorship involving obscenity or sex as are most of the laws in our country today. Literature was censored then because it was considered dangerous to the political or religious power of a ruler. Thus, when the Church of Rome undertook the censorship of books in the fourth century A.D. in Carthage, it was not to protect the people from any "filth" in writing, but from anti-religious works. At that time the Church issued a decree forbidding Christians to circulate or possess any writings of the old pagans—the "unbelievers."

As the Roman Empire crumbled, what education and culture remained within the area was supervised by the Church, which in many cases was also the government. Book production was limited to what could be copied by hand and much of this work, in the Middle Ages, was done by monks. As a result, the books that were preserved usually dealt with religious, philosophical, or scientific subjects acceptable to the Church.

Printing, invented in China perhaps as early as the ninth century, was not introduced to Europe until the fifteenth century. From that time, however, the development of the book and of book printing was very rapid. By the sixteenth century, the art and skill of bookmaking had reached great heights, and bookselling emerged as a sizeable business. The Church, not unaware of the wide influence books could now wield, began to take even stronger interest in their content.

The earliest known list of censored books was that drawn up by Charles V in Belgium in 1524, under Church advice. Less than two decades later an elaborate list of prohibited books—those considered heretical, or anti-Church —was issued at Venice. The religious faculty in Paris also drew up an Index and levied heavy penalties on such books. The Church was assisted in these endeavors by the faculties of the medieval universities, which had tremendous censorship powers, and which, in reality, were controlled by the Church: Oxford and Cambridge in England, the Sorbonne in Paris, the Berlin Academy of Sciences in Prussia, the University of Padua in the Venetian Republic, the University of Munich in Bavaria.

In England, Church influence lessened somewhat when the universities turned control of censorship over to a stationers' company. This company was to curtail "mischievous printers and authors." A few years later the English government took over the licensing of printed matter. It wasn't until the beginning of the seventeenth century, however, that censorship in England began to turn its direction away from works of religious or political import to those considered "indelicate" or "obscene."

Certain European intellectuals were beginning to write in the popular tongues of their nations. Galileo, for example, wrote in Latin, the educated man's language, at the beginning of his career, but when he decided he wanted to reach a larger audience, he wrote in Italian. So it was in England, too. And as the number of books grew, so the variety increased. Anglo-Saxons were very forthright people (see the *Canterbury Tales,* unexpurgated) and they wrote forthrightly, liberally using "four-letter words" referring to physical processes and parts of the body in their books.

With the spread of literacy in England, it was inevitable that censors would broaden their bases to include those works considered "obscene," those works which, in their view, threatened public morality. And in dealing with such matters the common law that was developed was to become the precedent for Americans to follow. This common law was so called because it was common to all England, as opposed to laws covering only a specific locality or area. Common law did not embody existing statutes, but rather was created by various judges in various cases.

In 1725 in England a judge ruled that it was a crime to publish obscenity. Richard Curl was convicted on the basis of a volume he issued called *Venue in the Cloister, or The Nun in Her Smock.* Appeals were made to other courts, but the conviction was upheld. Forty-odd years later John Wilkes was prosecuted on the basis of this decision for a supposedly obscene poem, *Essay on Women.*

By the late eighteenth century, the power of the Church in most European countries had been seriously curtailed. In England, the struggles of Cromwell and the Stuarts were long over and the established Church was in ascendance, but during the seventeenth and eighteenth centuries a body of common law had developed which removed much of the Church's power over the individual.

On American shores, although many of the early colonists established theocratic settlements, the Federal Constitution adopted in 1788 specifically separated Church and State and gave no secular power to the Church whatsoever, nor any recognition of any church or any religion as special in nature.

Within three years, in 1791, nine amendments—the Bill of Rights—were added to the U.S. Constitution to insure sufficient quantities of individual liberties. The First Amendment, which has figured so prominently in many legal actions involving censorship, specifically stated that "Congress shall make no law respecting an establishment of religion, or prohibiting the free exercise thereof; or abridging the freedom of speech or of the press. . . ."

Some say that the First Amendment was drawn so that the states would always retain their right to control individual freedoms, and so that the national government, through the institution of Congress, could not usurp those powers. Although this may or may not have been the intent of the founding fathers, the federal government in this country today, through the U.S. Supreme Court, has final say in censorship matters. States may pass laws, but the final determination of cases brought before the local or state judicial bodies still remains, through appeal, with the national court.

One of the great difficulties in dealing with censorship in this country involves the legal interpretation of the word "obscene." According to Webster's dictionary, it means: "1. offensive to modesty or decency; lewd. 2. disgusting; filthy; repulsive." Yet, throughout the history of cultural censorship in this country, as community standards have changed, so have the interpretation of what is "offensive to modesty or decency" and the meaning of the words "lewd, disgusting, filthy, and repulsive." What was considered obscene a hundred years ago is accepted without a tremor by most people today. What is now considered to be obscene may be thoroughly acceptable in the next century.

It is instructive, however, if not always amusing, to follow the efforts on behalf of cultural censorship in America. Sometimes these attempts are direct, by laws of governments; sometimes groups or individuals try to be the censors; and sometimes censorship is so subtle that it is barely detectable.

CHAPTER 3

The Crusader

THE BIGGEST field for the cultural censor in the modern world has always been that of the written word, and especially the world of books. Yet the first obscenity case in the United States did not involve a book, but a picture.

In 1815, in Philadelphia, Jesse Sharpless, along with several associates, was convicted of exhibiting a "certain lewd, wicked, scandalous, infamous, and obscene painting, representing a man in an obscene, impudent, and indecent posture with a woman, to the manifest corruption and subversion of youth, and other citizens . . . against the peace and dignity of the commonwealth. . . ."

The judges were not even allowed to see the picture for fear of "wounding . . . eyes or ears." The painting was subsequently held to tend "to the manifest corruption of youth and other citizens. . . ." For the first time in the United States, judicial steps had been taken to protect its peoples against the obscene.

Six years later came the first obscenity case against a

book. The book was the famous *Fanny Hill* by John Cleland, which had been published in England in the 1740s and had long been outlawed there. It was published in America by Peter Holmes, under the title *Memoirs of a Woman of Pleasure*. This book about the life of a prostitute was decreed to be "lewd, wicked, scandalous, infamous, and obscene. . . ." Here again the judge, Isaac Parker, chief judge of the Massachusetts Supreme Court, did not see the material. To do so, he said, would be "to require that the public itself should give permanency and notoriety to indecency, in order to punish it."

These first cases were tried under the common law, for no statutes existed which prohibited the publishing of obscene material. Judges in each case made the decisions, which then became part of the common law. At about this time, however, the states became interested in seeing that their citizens were not corrupted by "indecent" literature. With the increased education of the populace, and the growth in the number and variety of publications that were appearing throughout the country, there seemed to many to be a threat to the morals of the people.

Vermont led the way with an anti-indecency statute in 1821; Connecticut was next; then came Massachusetts in 1835. That same year the federal government, concerned that slaves might possibly be incited to rebellion by materials sent through the mail, put before Congress a proposal to bar all such material from being sent through the federal postal system. Senators Clay, Calhoun, and Webster spoke out to claim that such a law would be a violation of the Constitution. They reminded Congress that President George Washington had proposed that there be no charge for delivery of mail, because he believed that the federal government—if paid for the service—might try to control its content. Even if the federal government took care of the mailing, the Senators claimed, the government had no right to censor the contents. The bill was defeated.

After the middle of the nineteenth century, the "problem" of obscenity received widespread public attention, largely through the flamboyant efforts of a ginger-whiskered, stocky upholder of purity, who in his own words saw himself "stationed in a swamp at the mouth of a sewer." The man was Anthony Comstock, and his name was eventually to become a household word.

Born in 1844 in New Canaan, Connecticut, Anthony Comstock was a thoughtful and religious young man. As a boy he liked to go hunting for squirrels, chipmunks, and rabbits. He enlisted in the Union Army during the Civil War to take the place of his older brother who had been killed at Gettysburg. It was in the camp barracks that he first indicated his disapproval of the actions and thoughts of others. He wrote in his diary that a "feeling of sadness" came over him when he heard the other men. "It seems as though I should sink when I heard the air resounding with the oaths of wicked men." For comfort he turned to a book of hymns.

After his service in the army he had various odd jobs, including that of clerk and bookkeeper in a grocery store in New Haven, Connecticut, and then finally he went to New York City with only $5 in his pockets. There he found a job with a drygoods company and spent lonely evenings of prayer in a cheap lodging house. Comstock looked around him and did not like what he saw. His business associates were interested in "erotic books and pictures." He was also distressed by the violations of the Sunday closing law by certain saloons in his neighborhood. When the police officer Comstock had called to close them did not act, Comstock took matters into his own hands:

"I am determined to act the part of a good citizen and wherever a man breaks the laws I will make him satisfy the laws' demands, if in my power." Comstock brought charges against the saloonkeepers before the police commissioners. His crusade had begun.

Comstock had a precedent for his single-minded, single-handed early efforts to protect his fellow citizens from being exposed to lust and lewdness: one Thomas Bowdler, a doctor in England. Dr. Bowdler's talent was to expurgate, or cut, literature, and his prize product was *The Family Shakespear.*

In truth, most of the Bowdler family had been expurgators. They grew up in an era when delicacy was of prime importance in English life. As a Reverend John Bennett wrote in 1789, "Delicacy is a very general and comprehensive quality. It extends to everything where woman is concerned. Conversation, books, pictures, attitude, gesture, pronunciation should all come under its salutary restraints. . . . A girl should hear, she should see, nothing that can call forth a blush, or even stain the purity of her mind."

This view was accepted in the society of the time and even flourished for a period. Then in the nineteenth century, with the rise of literacy, the reading public expanded. Gentlemen such as Dr. Bowdler felt that the new masses of readers had to be protected from the indelicate. His father, an aristocratic man, had set the pattern years before. He "bowdlerized" orally when reading to the assembled family members. Such was his good taste, that his son once wrote that they all listened with delight to Shakespeare "without knowing that those matchless tragedies contained expressions improper to be pronounced and without having any reason to suspect that any parts of the plays had been omitted by the circumspect and judicious reader." Those evenings of reading, the good doctor said, were the inspirations for his *The Family Shakespear.*

Actually, the first edition of *The Family Shakespear,* published in 1807, was edited by Dr. Bowdler's sister, Harriet, who was a very proper woman, high-minded and intellectual. *She* never saw the dancers in operas she attended. She kept her eyes shut because it was so indelicate that she could not bear to look.

Miss Bowdler also felt that Shakespeare was most indelicate and needed a very proper pruning. Through careful editing, out went any profanity, any indelicacy, any blasphemy. Some surmised that Harriet did not claim the editorship of the first *Family Shakespear* because it might have been most indelicate on her part to admit that she, a woman of fifty, and an unmarried one at that, understood Shakespeare's obscenities well enough to delete them. In any case, Dr. Bowdler soon joined or took over from his sister and a second edition of *The Family Shakespear* appeared, with his name as editor, in 1817. In a few years the book was a best seller, perhaps because it so fittingly suited the temper of the times.

As the Bowdlers had devoted themselves to purifying literature for readers in England, now in America in the nineteenth century came the bull-necked, blustering Anthony Comstock. But unlike the Bowdlers, he would not change the written word. He would prevent the written word from being published; he would see to it that it was banned from the readers.

Interestingly enough, Comstock too came on the scene at a time when there was a spirit of social consciousness in the air. The Civil War was over; urban centers showed great growth. Intelligent leaders of the community were pressing for social reforms. Anthony Comstock fit into the picture.

He seized the initiative to crusade against sin, and swept up into his campaign some of the most prominent men in America.

In 1865 Congress adopted a law attempting to keep obscenity from the mails. The law stated that mailing obscene publications would be a criminal offense. If something obscene was sent through the mail, then the offender could be fined and/or jailed. But as the Post Office did not have the right to censor material before it was mailed—the recipient had first to complain—there were not very many prosecutions. Three years later, the New York state legislature passed a bill for the suppression of "obscene literature," largely at the instigation of the YMCA of New York, which had determined that in that city young men showed an alarming weakness for poker and prostitutes and for "vile weekly newspapers" and "licentious books."

Comstock was delighted. Now he had a state law to back him in his work. He spent all of his spare time from business seeing that dealers of magazines or books that he deemed unsuitable were arrested. By 1872, however, he came to the conclusion that there was need for a federal law so that he could have the publishers prosecuted instead of just the dealers. Knowing the YMCA would view that idea with enthusiasm, Comstock suggested that they join forces in an effort to get passage of such a federal law. They did so, and formed the Committee for the Suppression of Vice, with Comstock as its agent.

The results were swift and gratifying. The next year the committee received a charter from the New York legislature, becoming the New York Society for the Suppression of Vice. It gained the support of such influential men as banker J. Pierpont Morgan, copper magnate William E. Dodge, and soapmaker Samuel Colgate. In addition, the federal government, as a result of the lobbying by Comstock and his society, passed a new law, much stricter and more detailed, regulating the sending of "obscene or crime-inciting matter" through the mails. This obscenity law, which became known as the Comstock Law, declared nonmailable matter "every obscene, lewd, lascivious, or filthy book, pamphlet, picture, paper, letter, writing, print, or other publication of an indecent character" along with all articles, drugs, medicine concerned with "preventing conception or producing abortion" or any other written matter pertaining to the same. The fine was "not more than $5,000 or imprisonment not more than five years, or both, for the first offense. . . ."

Comstock was appointed a special agent of the Post Office with police power. There was no more time for business as he knew it at his job. He quit, and his full-time business now became the pursuit of purveyors of sinful material.

Heady with power, Comstock set about his tasks with fervor. The Society reported in 1873 that during the first year of its existence, its secretary and general agent (Comstock) was "assaulted and stabbed almost fatally by representatives of the traffic in obscenity." But Comstock was not a man to be intimidated. In its 1874 report, the Society stated that since March, 1872, "130,000 pounds of bound books" had been seized, as had "60,300 articles made of rubber for immoral purposes. . . ." All seizures were followed by total destruction of property. And Mr. Comstock, "in prosecution of the work, has travelled by railroad 23,500 miles." The Society's work was "just begun," but it was important, Comstock emphasized, for "a single book or a single picture may taint forever the soul of the person who reads or sees it."

In the next few years, sparked by the success of the New York Society, similar groups sprang up throughout the

country, and laws similar to the 1873 federal obscenity law
were passed by state after state. There came in Boston the
New England Watch and Ward Society, then a vice suppression society in Philadelphia, one in Cincinnati, in Cleveland, in St. Louis, Louisville, Chicago, in Rochester, Providence, Detroit, Toledo, San Francisco, and Portland.

The New York Society was kept busy not only with literature. They raided the gambling place of "the notorious
Al Adams." By 1889 eleven tons of gambling material had
been seized and destroyed. They opposed the "degrading
shows" at the Chicago World's Fair in 1893. They "res-
cued" girls from "disorderly houses."

The members and supporters of the vice societies were
now riding high, backed by law in their efforts to "uplift"
their society by driving out the "impure." That they were
able during this period to be successful was in part due to
the fact that the intelligent, aristocratic, moneyed mer-
chants, bankers, financiers, businessmen, philanthropists, all
approved of their aims and lent such support as they could,
which often was considerable. Three hundred "leading citizens" signed a petition in favor of cleaning up the literature
sold in railway stations. It was sent to all New England railroad stations by the Watch and Ward Society, which had
embarked upon a campaign against crime books and "degrading" magazines such as *The Police Gazette*, which contained pictures of scantily clad women. So influential were
the petitioners, that the offending literature was immediately removed.

The vice societies obtained convictions under the federal law and heavy fines against booksellers. Their censorship activities drew high praise, and were often grouped
with those of other do-gooders, such as those who worked
for prison reform or poor relief. Everyone, it seemed, was
for purity and progress.

Most of the public efforts at censorship in the late nineteenth century were directed at books considered vulgar and degrading, and of course, "obscene, lewd, lascivious, or filthy." Generally these were little known works, for the respectable book publishers seemed to have the same ideas as the vice-hunters and policed their own ranks by not choosing to publish the offensive. When the Watch and Ward Society prodded a Boston district attorney into complaining about a planned edition of *Leaves of Grass* by Walt Whitman, there was no struggle. The publisher, James R. Osgood, cancelled his contract with the author.

Such books, even when published, rarely found their way onto library shelves, for many librarians took strong stands as to which books should be made available to the public. They generally supported those who would censor; in 1908, the president of the American Library Association, Arthur Bostwick, urged the suppression of all books of an "immoral tendency."

As the years went on, Comstock became shrilly vocal about the lust caused by books, declaring that lust was "the boon companion" of all other crimes. "Lust defiles the body, debauches the imagination, corrupts the will, destroys the memory, sears the conscience, hardens the heart and damns the soul," he cried.

Although Comstock continued to convict persons and destroy book plates, toward the end of the nineteenth century criticism of his zeal and motives was beginning to appear. Some of the newspapers began to treat him as a common joke because of his gaudy raids and emotional tirades, even though Comstock had wielded his power in far-flung arenas, including museums from which he took "some loads of anatomical filthiness."

When Comstock was at the peak of his power he inspired a new derisive phrase about censorship. In 1905

George Bernard Shaw had written a play, *Mrs. Warren's Profession,* which had been banned from the British stage (England had precensorship) because the play dealt with prostitution. Comstock announced that if anyone dared to put the play on stage in the United States he would prosecute. Some sources say Comstock referred to Shaw as "the Irish smut-dealer," others that he called Shaw "a foreign writer of filth." No matter, the play was produced in New York, and Comstock did prosecute, to no avail. The New York court ruled that Shaw's play did not fall within the scope of the New York state obscenity law. George Bernard Shaw's comment was: "Comstockery!"

Although Comstock was exposed to jibes by some, faithfully and exuberantly he continued to carry out his censorship work until his death in 1915. After forty years' service in the "fight against obscenity," he had, he said, "convicted persons enough to fill a passenger train of 61 coaches, 60 coaches containing 60 passengers each, and the sixty-first almost full . . . and destroyed over 160 tons of obscene literature."

It was a measure of how closely in tune he was with the temper and spirit of his times that the notice of his death called forth fulsome praise. The *New York Times* spoke of him as a "benefactor and a hero." He had "served a good cause with tireless devotion." The *Outlook* stated that the "warfare he was waging was much more important than his blunders of taste. . . ." The *New Republic* admitted that from time to time Comstock had "conspicuously made an ass of himself," but that he also had done a "vast amount of good."

Yet other voices were heard, and in spite of the efforts of the vice societies and the country's other upholders of morals, the passing of the years brought fewer and fewer convictions and a general weakening of the societies' influence. Partly due to the pressures exerted by the many reform groups that were active, the public was now beginning to discuss issues, sex among them, that had never had airing before. In the efforts to eliminate vice, for example, there was much talk about prostitution. How then could one rationally prosecute books that dealt with prostitution, books that were a favorite target of Comstock and others?

One case in particular was indicative of the changing mood. Comstock had, shortly before his death, found a certain novel about two shopgirls to be completely "rotten." The book was a morality tale, *Hagar Revelly*. The author was Daniel Carson Goodman, a doctor, and he had written the book as a moral lesson about vice. (One girl stayed pure, the other became wayward, to say the least.) Comstock secured an indictment, led a force of U.S. marshals, and raided the publisher's office. The publisher, Mitchell Kennerley, was arrested. Previously a clerk had already been convicted in a New York state court for selling the book. Now Kennerley was to be tried in a federal court in New York. Although he was convicted because of the precedents established through the years and by the past interpretations of obscenity, the federal judge, Learned Hand, commented that while the obscenity law was in tune with "mid-Victorian morals," it did not seem to him to answer to "the understanding and morality of the present time, as conveyed by the words, 'obscene, lewd, or lascivious.'" Judge Hand was indicating that morals—and literature—changed with the times.

He went on to say, "I question whether in the end men will regard that as obscene which is honestly relevant to the adequate expression of innocent ideas, and whether they will not believe that truth and beauty are too precious to society at large to be mutilated in the interests of those most likely to pervert them to base uses. Indeed, it seems hardly likely that we are . . . to be content to reduce our treatment of sex to the standard of a child's library in the supposed interest of a salacious few. . . ."

Judge Hand did not dismiss the charge against Kennerley, but because he expressed doubts about the soundness of the precedents for the case, it went to the Federal Court of Appeals. And there, Kennerley was acquitted.

CHAPTER 4

The Judges and Censorship

A F T E R Anthony Comstock's death, John S. Sumner, a lawyer, became head of the New York Society for the Suppression of Vice. Sumner lacked the dash of Comstock, but not the devotion to duty. A few months after he took over, he was successful in having the plates destroyed on a rather obscure book, *Homo Sapiens*, written by Polish author Stanislaw Przybskewski and published by Alfred A. Knopf. Either by intimidation or court proceedings, Sumner was determined to squelch what he considered impure or obscene literature.

Then came World War I, which gave the vice societies new confidence, for in the pursuit of the war there seemed to be a spirit of moral uplift everywhere. Americans were fighting and dying for America in Europe, the enemy was wicked, the allied forces were righteous. Citizens were urged to keep their communities clean. Officials in this country worried about loose moral behavior around military camps. Congress appropriated four million dollars to combat prostitution and venereal disease. John Sumner went to

France with the YMCA to help uphold morals there. Everywhere he talked about the good and the pure, and warned his listeners to beware of the impure. Then he came home to talk some more.

The public was aroused. In 1917 twelve states introduced bills controlling obscene literature. Pressure groups passionately promoted loyalty, patriotism, and virtue, and the drive for the prohibition of liquor took on added force. Librarians sought to blacklist books that were pacifist or morbid.

Sadly for the vice crusaders, however, the end of the war did not bring a permanent continuance of moral uplift. In the peacetime readjustment that followed, Victorian attitudes seemed outmoded, and though John Sumner declared that American literature should radiate "joy and adventure," new writers and new publishers were exploring new fields. Free, frank novels from Europe were for the first time extensively translated and published in the United States. And once the general tide had turned, there was little the vice societies could do to stem it.

They tried. In 1920 they instigated the seizure by police of the printing plates, unbound sheets, and copies of *Jurgen* by Branch Cabell, a novel which *New York Tribune* columnist Heywood Broun had called a "nasty . . . barroom story refurbished for the boudoir." The case languished in the courts for several years, then a new defense attorney won an acquittal for the publishers, and the judge called the book "brilliant" and of "unusual literary merit."

From then on the more cases the vice societies brought to court, the more failures they seemed to have. For they were now attacking not only little known works, but the whole spectrum of the then-contemporary literature. Even books from respected publishers were under their surveillance. The New York Society's reports in the twenties recorded their activities against "the mass of sex-perverted, so-called literature that some publishers are pouring upon our market."

More and more the vice societies were on the defensive, denying the charge of censorship. After one raid on a publishing house, confiscating an entire edition of a novel, a New York newspaper was prompted to editorialize: "Censorship is an evil thing anywhere and at any time. But it is at its worst in the hands of the Sumners."

Judges began dismissing charges brought against publishers, and worse, the offended parties began filing damage suits against the vice societies! But the more setbacks these groups had, the more determined they were not to lose their control, which, though lessening, was still considerable. The New York Society and Sumner began to feel that their recent failures in the courts were due to too weak an obscenity law.

From the time that the first case involving an "obscene" book was heard in Massachusetts, the various courts and judges had been plagued by interpretations about the meaning, scope, and applications of the obscenity laws. Not surprisingly, early American judicial thought on these questions relied heavily on British precedent.

The first legal definition of "obscenity" was made in England in 1868. A pamphlet criticizing the Confessional of the Roman Church had been declared by a British lower court as not falling within the obscenity act because it had not been published for the single purpose of corrupting the morals of youth. The Lord Chief Justice, Sir Alexander Cockburn, disagreed. He overruled the lower court, saying: "I think the test of obscenity is this, whether the tendency of the matter charged as obscenity is to deprave and corrupt those whose minds are open to such immoral influences and into whose hands a publication of this sort may fall." By this definition any book that might have some evil effect on anyone was declared criminal.

In the first such case before the United States Supreme Court, the Rosen case in 1896, the trial judge was to charge the jury in almost the very same words that Cockburn had used. Lew Rosen had published a twelve-page paper, *Broadway*. What was unusual about the paper was that if one applied a piece of bread to a page, a picture which was hitherto invisible, covered by lampblack, would appear. Rosen claimed that the pictures were "innocent hilarity." The prosecution called them "females in different attitudes of indecency," and thus nonmailable, and the court agreed. However, the defendant was never told specifically in the charges against him exactly what matter in his paper was deemed obscene.

Although the Rosen case was widely quoted in the legal arguments of many obscenity cases that followed, judicial groping continued for definite standards by which written material could be suppressed or allowed. In another case before the Supreme Court that year, the judges declared that while the defendant's material was vulgar (it was a libelous attack upon another man), it did not come under the obscenity law. The judges stated that the words "obscene," "lewd," and "lascivious," as used in the law, signified that form of immorality which had relation to sexual impurity. As the material in this case did not pertain to sex, it was thus ruled not to be "obscene."

Other judicial views were brought out in a case in 1917 when the New York Society for the Suppression of Vice managed to bring to court a bookstore clerk named Raymond D. Halsey. Halsey was charged with selling to an

agent of the Society a copy of *Mademoiselle de Maupin* by
Théophile Gautier, a prominent French writer of the nineteenth century. Although the judges conflicted in their
views, the book clerk was acquitted, the book was not
deemed obscene or indecent, and the clerk sued to recover
damages for malicious prosecution. But the significance of
the case lay not in the final decision but in the proceedings
that led to it. The book was considered as a whole, not just
by a few paragraphs; testimony from literary experts both
then living and dead was offered in defense of the work; and
the reputation of the author was considered. From that time
on, there were many exhortations for "opinion testimony"
in deciding whether a work was obscene or not, but even by
the 1920s there was still no clear legal or judicial definition
of the word "obscene."

The New York Society, faced with more frequent setbacks in the courts, decided that a stronger definition was
needed. In the mid-twenties, a Clean Books League was
formed to lobby for stricter legislation, and an amendment
to sharpen the teeth of the existing New York state obscenity law was introduced. This amendment provided that an
obscenity indictment could be based upon any part of a
book and that only this part could be admitted in evidence.
Further, books that were "filthy" and "disgusting" in any
manner could be suppressed, even if they were not sexually
stimulating. Trial had to be by jury in obscenity cases, and
the introduction of expert testimony in obscenity trials "for
any purpose whatsoever" was forbidden.

The campaign to pass the amendment nearly suc-
ceeded, for many influential persons, including some publishers, supported the move, and opposition was not immediately vocal. One essayist called literary censorship a
"moral preservation that saves right-minded people from

being thrown into a cesspool of immorality." A Harvard professor said the rash of "unclean books" was a "clear and present danger." An elderly bookseller said there should be sold "nothing but wholesome books." A businessman said that there was "nothing in the world the businessman wants more than a clean book." Librarians debated. Some said they should bring to all the people the books that belong to them. Others complained about the appearance of so many novels of "neurotic exploration." And the *Literary Digest* poll found that "the generality" favored "some form of censorship."

Then the reaction set in. Opponents of the New York bill began to become active. Publishers and politicians raised their voices, warning of the dangers of censorship. At its test, the bill failed, thirty-one senators against, fifteen in favor.

The New York Society for the Suppression of Vice desperately redoubled its efforts, still hoping to get the bill passed in a new legislative campaign. But the public had turned against it, and the Clean Books crusade was doomed. No new amendments were made to the New York state obscenity law.

The failure of their legislative campaign was a blow to the vice societies. Their defeats in the courts continued, their power waned. In 1929 the New York Society was able to report that it had destroyed $20,000 worth of books that year, all burned by the order of the district attorney. But it was also in 1929 that John Sumner lost what was perhaps his most publicized case.

The Well of Loneliness, a novel by Radclyffe Hall, had been published in England in 1928. Based largely on its author's own experiences, it won immediate praise from English critics for its honesty and sensitivity. But because it dealt with a very delicate subject—that of the lesbian—the novel was soon found to be legally obscene. An American publisher had planned an edition of the book, but after its suppression in England decided against such a move.

However, a small house, Covici-Friede, was not so timid, and an American edition was published. John Sumner immediately purchased a copy of the book, and police followed through with the arrest. The case was brought into the magistrate's court in New York City in February, 1929, and Friede was found guilty. The judge declared the book to be indeed of literary merit, but harking back to the old Cockburn view, also said the work must be tested as to whether the tendency was "to deprave or corrupt those whose minds are open to such immoral influences. . . ." The judge was convinced that *The Well of Loneliness* did tend "to debauch public morals," and that "its subject matter is offensive to public decency. . . ." This was because, the judge indicated, "the unnatural and depraved relationships portrayed are sought to be idealized and extolled. The characters . . . are described in attractive terms. . . ."

Friede appealed his case, and later that year a higher court of three judges ruled that the book was not obscene, thus establishing that a book could not be banned on the sole basis of its theme. The Society had lost, and in more ways than one. The practical result of the trials was that the publicity aroused unusual interest in the book. Over 100,000 copies were sold within a year.

The New York Society was indeed falling upon evil days, but no more so than others elsewhere in the country. The Illinois Vigilance Association, after years of raiding speakeasies and fighting for pure books, caused the arrest of nine Chicago booksellers. The exposure of their methods of entrapping booksellers by the use of agents (who bought suspect books and even badgered booksellers into especially ordering them) aroused sentiment against the organization, and its head was denounced by a jury as an "un-American snooper."

Perhaps the Watch and Ward Society in Boston became the most thoroughly discredited group of all. Its early years of operation were certainly less flamboyant than those of the New York Society. While New York do-gooders were noisily protesting one book after another, the Boston group was quietly going about its work. It had set up a Boston Bookseller's Committee, a group of gentlemanly booksellers and several Watch and Warders. The committee read and judged the then current novels. If they gave approval, the booksellers in the city could sell the book, with the confidence that they would not be prosecuted. If they disapproved of a book, all sellers were notified, and warned they would be prosecuted within forty-eight hours of any sale of the book. The system was effective for a time, for it was a quiet, orderly procedure of censorship. Occasionally a few booksellers chafed at the control but the public was not alarmed until a very noisy case splashed on the scene. This case, and some which followed, catapulted Boston into the limelight, and the slogan "Banned in Boston" soon was heard throughout the nation.

Henry L. Mencken, publisher of *American Mercury* magazine, and the Watch and Ward Society had been at odds for some time. Appearing in the magazine were scornful attacks on the Society. J. Frank Chase, the Watch and Ward head, smarted at the insults, and finally had what he thought was a sure chance to strike back at Mencken. In 1926 the magazine published a story, "Hatrack," about a small town prostitute who found that she was publicly castigated, but privately held in favor by the noble citizens of the town. Chase announced to the magazine distributors that the sale of that issue of *American Mercury* would be subject to legal action. All newsstand dealers seemed to have heard the message, for the magazine disappeared from public view. One dealer, however, did not comply and was arrested.

Mencken decided to take matters into his own hands. In a public display in front of a crowd of about some 5,000 persons, at the foot of Boston Common, he formally sold Chase a copy of the condemned magazine. Mencken was arrested, but to the dismay of the Watch and Warders, was found not guilty by the judge. And the matter did not end there. Mencken's lawyer filed suit to keep the Watch and Ward Society and news dealers from harassing the *American Mercury.*

Again Mencken was the victor, for an injunction was issued. The judge called the tactics used in the "Hatrack" case "clearly illegal." Because Mencken was a zestful and forceful personality, news about the case spread all over the country, and the Society was severely shaken by both the reverses and by all the unpleasant publicity that attended them.

Surprisingly, the decline in influence of the Watch and Warders did not bring a corresponding decline in censorship. Others merely stepped in to fill the breach. Catholic bishops and clergy in Boston, as a result of the 1927 Vatican pronouncements against immoral literature, attempted to impose the Church's views on what should be made available to readers. The police began to be active in arresting sellers of books they deemed immoral. Obvious excesses began to occur. Booksellers were warned that the sale of Sinclair Lewis's *Elmer Gantry* would be grounds for prosecution. Boston banned *An American Tragedy* by Theodore

Dreiser. The sale of *Oil,* a novel about the Harding administration scandals by Upton Sinclair, brought about a bookseller's arrest. (*Oil* contained a reference to birth control.)

The Watch and Ward Society had one last noisy fling
against D. H. Lawrence's *Lady Chatterley's Lover,* which
was to thoroughly arouse the anti-censorship forces. Again
the Society had entrapped a bookseller, this time in Cambridge, Massachusetts, persuading him to sell the offending
work. The bookstore proprietor, James A. De Lacey, who
was respected by Harvard students and faculty alike, was
convicted of selling obscene material. But though the
Watch and Ward Society won a victory, it lost the battle.
Public sympathy was with De Lacey, and there was widespread revulsion against the Society's methods. An aroused
public, who were becoming tired of the ridicule heaped
upon Boston for its repressive censorship, worked for and
won acceptance of a liberalizing amendment to the state's
obscenity law. Little was heard from the Watch and Ward
Society from that time on.

Within the United States, cases concerning books continued to be tried in the courts, but by the end of the
twenties, both the public and the authorities had begun to
focus their attention elsewhere—on magazines.

A whole new group of periodicals had arisen, threatening the established publications such as the *Literary Digest,*
the *Woman's Home Companion,* and *Collier's.* Some called
these new magazines—*True Confessions, Modern Ro-
mances,* etc.—"gutter literature," and the respected magazines and newspapers began to speak out about the "filth"
of the "pulps." So much public attention was called to this
"immoral and harmful literature" that dozens of pressure
groups, temperance, religious, pacifist, and women's groups
among them, initiated campaigns against "bad" magazines.

One Congressional representative from Mississippi went even further. He introduced a bill in 1927 that proposed the formation of a National Board of Magazine Censorship. He listed over sixty magazines as "vile" publications—and among them were the highly regarded *Harper's Bazaar* and *Vanity Fair*. Another Congressman, this time from the state of Washington, introduced his own bill to control magazines the following year. Neither piece of proposed legislation, however, progressed further than committees.

Magazines could be kept from potential readers by local pressures upon, or arrests of, newspaper dealers who sold them, or by control by the federal postal department, which could ban materials from the mails under a section of its postal code that dealt with obscenity. (This was the old law that Anthony Comstock had been so instrumental in getting adopted by Congress back in 1873.)

The federal government had two very important means of censoring the written word: the postal code in reference to mailing, and the long-established powers of the United States Customs Bureau. In 1842, a customs law had been passed to keep undesirable foreign "daguerreotypes and photographs" from entering the country. In truth, however, it had been used through the years to prohibit the entrance of any publications deemed obscene or otherwise undesirable. Customs officials simply destroyed them at the ports of entry.

The enforcement of this law in practice made the local officials the censors of literature to be imported to the United States. The local inspector decided whether a book was acceptable or not. He could be overruled by an appeal to the U.S. Customs Court in New York City, but that did not often happen. In addition, the Treasury Department also reviewed the customs decisions. As a result, a book could be banned as obscene at one port, passed through at another. It could be judged one way by the U.S. Customs Court, another by Treasury officials in Washington. So great did the confusion become that in 1928 lawyers from the Customs Bureau and the Post Office department got together and drew up a list of over 700 books (among them books by Balzac, Ovid, Joyce, and D. H. Lawrence) that could not be imported, or could not be mailed within the country.

In the spring of 1929, when the customs bill came up for reconsideration, there was much discussion in Congress about the section that dealt with the importation of books. An amendment was proposed which would include as non-importable books those advocating "treason, insurrection or forcible resistance to any law of the United States. . . ." A Pandora's box was opened, and heated discussions ensued. Senator Bronson Cutting of New Mexico attacked not only the proposed "treason" amendment, but the whole section of the tariff bill dealing with the importation of literature as being "unsound." He challenged the wisdom of letting customs officials "dictate what the American people may or may not read."

There was much public discussion of the issues, too, and the result was that the amendment which was finally passed brought about a liberalization of the customs law. In the past an "obscene" book from abroad had been destroyed—in effect, precensorship. Now decisions relating to books were subject to review by judges and juries. And a book was to be judged as a whole, not just on the basis of an "obscene" portion. The Treasury was given an option to let in books it considered to be "classics." The law as amended now provided that the authorities could proceed against the book itself instead of against the person who published, bought, or sold it.

Thus it was that James Joyce's *Ulysses* came to the attention of the courts in the United States. The book had long been in legal difficulties, ever since its first publication in Paris in 1922. U.S. Customs officials had time and time again burned copies of the book. Now in 1933, a copy of the book had been ordered imported by a publisher who proposed to print the book in the United States. As expected, the book was seized, and the case brought to court. Judge John M. Woolsey reported he found *Ulysses* a "sincere and serious attempt to devise a new literary method for the observation and description of mankind," and decreed that the book could be admitted into the United States. Judge Woolsey was not alarmed by the use of "four-letter" words, which "are criticized as dirty . . . but are old Saxon words known to almost all men. . . ." The government did appeal the case to a higher court, and there the decision was upheld. These judges called *Ulysses* "a book of originality and sincerity of treatment" and concluded it did not have the "effect of promoting lust." Thus *Ulysses* was importable and was published in the United States.

There were other struggles through the years, both with books and magazines. *Life* magazine in 1938 ran an article accompanied by stills from a motion picture, "The Birth of a Baby." Though the treatment of the subject was thoughtful and scientific, attacks were made upon the magazine by pressure groups and some sellers of the magazine were arrested. The publisher of *Life* chose to stand on the First Amendment, and further claimed that he was proud to have published the article. The case went to court. The defense, using an old technique, called in qualified witnesses, health authorities, welfare workers, and educators who testified in behalf of the article. The publisher was acquitted and the practice of offering testimony of informed witnesses was brought to public attention. Another victory had been won by the forces of cultural freedom.

CHAPTER 5

World War II and Afterward

THE DEPRESSION thirties witnessed the rise of repressive dictatorships in Spain, Germany, and Italy, and the Moscow trials under Stalin. There were public book burnings, suppression of publication of any material critical of those in power, suspension of guarantees of personal liberties for "the good of the State."

In the United States, however, there was little inclination for widespread censorship arrests or well-publicized court cases. Not until the forties, during and after World War II, did any spectacular occurrences of book censorship catch the public eye. In that period, as in World War I, there was again an urge for moral uplift.

One of the most interesting cases—that of a magazine —was to do much to limit the powers of the Post Office in matters of censorship. In line with the renewed emphasis on "purity," Postmaster General Steve Hannegan launched a campaign against what were called "girlie" magazines. Hannegan indicted these, not for obscenity, but because they failed in their "positive duty to contribute to the public good and public welfare."

In 1942 he rescinded the second-class mailing permit for *Esquire* magazine. He had called that permit a "certificate of good moral character." In reality, in order to obtain the second-class mailing rates, commercial material had only to sell a certain percentage of its print order and to be published for "the dissemination of information of a public character, or devoted to literature, the sciences, arts. . . ." The Postmaster General did not claim that the January to November 1943 issues of *Esquire* magazine were not mailable; he contended that they were neither devoted to "literature" nor "art," and therefore could not claim the subsidy of second-class matter.

Hannegan's ruling was upheld in a U.S. district court, was reversed in an appeals court, and finally reached the U.S. Supreme Court. There, the judges not only ruled that the Postmaster General had no right to bar *Esquire* from the mails, but went further. To uphold the revocation of the second-class privileges in this case, they said, would be to "grant the Postmaster General a power of censorship." They were sure that Congress, in framing the laws, had not intended to "clothe the Postmaster General with the power to supervise the tastes of the reading public of the country."

According to the Supreme Court, therefore, applicants for second-class permits did not have to convince the Postmaster General that their publications positively contributed to the public good or public welfare. The judges commented upon the wide varieties of tastes and ideas. "What is good literature, what has educational value, what is refined public information, what is good art, varies with individuals as it does from one generation to another. . . . A requirement that literature or art conform to some norm prescribed by an official smacks of an ideology foreign to our system. . . . What seems to one to be trash may have

for others fleeting or even enduring values. . . . To with-
draw the second-class rate from this publication today because its contents seemed to one official not good for the
public would sanction withdrawal of the second-class rate
tomorrow from another periodical whose social or economic
views seemed harmful to another official."

Thus this case pointed up the difficulties of relying
upon individual viewpoints—whether in the matter of
granting postal rates, or, extended, in interpretations as to
what the word "obscene" really means. Further, the Court,
by so supporting its verdict with judicial comments, defined
and narrowed the censorship powers of the Post Office.

In the late 1940s another case—one that did not reach
the U.S. Supreme Court—received much public attention.
The public was interested because it had bought over a million copies of the book in question: *Forever Amber* by Kathleen Winsor. This historical novel, set in England during the
Restoration, was prosecuted in Massachusetts in 1949. The
state attorney general felt that the book fell within the Massachusetts law concerning the "obscene, indecent, or impure." The publisher chose to defend the book, and the case
was tried by the state's highest court. The judges found that
it was unfortunate "that sexual episodes abound to the point
of tedium," but that the book had "historical purpose" and
did not "offend against the law."

In the 1950s, as the courts continued to judge the cases
brought to them, official censorship lessened, only to have
another form—unofficial censorship—arise to take its place.
These were the pressure groups: non-governmental bodies
of people who banded together to protect the public from
what they, the unofficial judges, deemed impure.

Private groups, prominent among them church-related
organizations, prepared blacklists and threatened and im-

posed general boycotts. In Oklahoma the American Legion forced a librarian out of her job solely because she sub-scribed to *The Nation*. In Chicago, the National Organiza-tion (later Office) for Decent Literature set up an office in 1955 to coordinate its efforts nationally "against the lascivi-ous type of literature which threatens moral, social, and na-tional life." NODL put pressure on news dealers, drug stores, and booksellers, to force them to remove from their stocks every item on the NODL blacklist. This list included books by Ernest Hemingway, William Faulkner, John Dos Passos, George Orwell, John O'Hara, and Émile Zola.

There were hundreds and hundreds of cases of such pressures and badgering. There was also resistance. The American Civil Liberties Union, which was opposed to cen-sorship of any kind, official or unofficial, made strenuous efforts to call attention to what it considered the impropri-ety of such actions. As a result of its efforts and those of other like-minded organizations, many book publishers fought back, and won their cases in the courts.

Not all censorship attempts were directed at "impure" literature. Minority groups were zealous to protect the im-ages of themselves that they considered to be realistic and proper. Other groups, however, were determined to protect the public from improper political ideas.

This period, the 1950s, was the time of the Cold War, the time when Russia and the United States viewed one an-other with suspicion. There was an air of fear in the coun-try, fear of Russia, and fear of Communism. This was the time of Congressional investigations into suspected Commu-nist subversion. Demagogues and publicity seekers came to the fore and aroused the public about the dangers of Com-munism in their country. Senator Joseph McCarthy capital-ized on and encouraged these fears, making a charge from the Senate floor that he had a list of over 200 names of "known Communists" working for the State Department—a list which he never produced, but which many people were eager to believe existed. McCarthyism soon infected the entire country. Politicians, writers, artists, entertainers —anyone in any walk of life who was suspected of being a "parlor pink" by McCarthy or his supporters—was black-listed.

At his peak, McCarthy attacked the United States International Information Administration (now the United States Information Agency) for having books in its libraries abroad which he claimed were written by Communist authors. The freedom to read in our libraries at home was also threatened, as pressure groups sought to have all controversial books removed from library shelves.

The librarians, to their great credit, almost uniformly resisted the pressures. They were supported in their views by President Dwight D. Eisenhower. At Dartmouth College on June 14, 1953, he warned: "Don't join the book-burners. Don't think you're going to conceal faults by concealing evidence that they ever existed. Don't be afraid to go to your library and read every book, as long as any document does not offend your own ideas of decency. That should be your only censorship."

Through these years the United States Supreme Court was faced with many questions concerning the federal obscenity law, including whether obscenity was protected by the First and Fourteenth Amendments, by our guaranteed freedoms of speech and press. In the past the Supreme Court had always assumed that it was not, but had abstained from voicing a direct opinion. In 1957, in the Roth case, the judges tried to clarify the issues. Justice William J. Brennan, Jr., who delivered the opinion of the Court, came to the conclusion that implicit in the history of the First Amendment was the rejection of obscenity as utterly without redeeming social importance, and that obscenity was thus not within the area of constitutionally protected speech or press.

Justice Brennan also clarified what "obscene" meant in the eyes of the Supreme Court. Sex and obscenity were not synonymous, he said; ". . . the test of obscenity is whether to the average person, applying contemporary community standards, the dominant theme of the material appeals to prurient interest."

Was *this* clarification? Various dictionaries provide various meanings for the word "prurient." A Webster dictionary defines it this way: "1. having lustful ideas or desires. 2. lustful, lascivious; lewd."

Had the judges really helped the various courts by giving a concrete guideline? It seemed not. In a California case two years later, a bookseller was convicted of selling an obscene book. When the case reached the Supreme Court, the bookseller was freed, because the Court decreed that he did not have knowledge of all the books in his store, and it was not reasonable to expect him to. One of the justices, Hugo Black, even wondered philosophically about the right of the Supreme Court to be involved with censorship as a whole.

Justice Black commented that the phrase in the First Amendment which read "no law . . . abridging the freedom of speech, or of the press" meant *no law abridging* and that the freedoms of speech and press were "beyond the Federal power to abridge." Further, he stated that the Supreme Court should not be the censor for the country (which it was, and is). "If, as it seems, we are on the way to national censorship, I think it timely to suggest again that there are grave doubts in my mind as to the desirability or constitutionality of this Court's becoming a Supreme Board of Censors—reading books and viewing television performances to determine whether, if permitted, they might adversely affect the morals of the people throughout the many diversified local communities in this vast country. . . . It is the duty of the courts to be watchful for the constitutional rights of the citizen, and against any stealthy encroachments thereon. While it is 'obscenity and indecency' before us today, the experience of mankind—both ancient and modern—shows that this type of elastic phrase can, and most likely will, be synonymous with the political, and maybe with the religious, unorthodoxy of tomorrow. Censorship is the deadly enemy of freedom and progress."

So the judges groped, in their continuing role of censor, to define the laws and guidelines for cultural censorship in the United States.

CHAPTER 6

"Smut" in the Sixties

THE CASE of *Lady Chatterley's Lover* by D. H. Lawrence is probably the most celebrated in the history of censorship in this country. Published in full for the first time in the United States by Grove Press in 1959, this book, which had been censored for years, contained a great number of four-letter words and explicit love scenes between Lady Chatterley and her husband's gamekeeper. The U.S. Post Office banned the book from the mails, contending that it offended contemporary community standards. The publisher challenged, and the case was heard in the lowest federal court, a district court.

The Supreme Court had previously decided that a writing was obscene or not depending on its effect on the average man according to contemporary standards. District Judge Frederick Van Pelt Bryan lifted the Post Office ban on the book, wondering in public how the Postmaster General could find that the book offended contemporary community standards. The book had been praised throughout the country, and yet, as Judge Bryan pointed out, the standards of a community could not be measured or ascertained accurately:

"Much of what is now accepted would have shocked the community to the core a generation ago. Today such things are generally tolerated whether we approve or not."

There was, indeed, he said, a "broadening of freedom of expression, and of the frankness with which sex and sex relations are dealt with at the present time which requires no discussion."

The appeals court agreed with Judge Bryan. However, one of the three judges there, Judge Leonard Moore, although reluctantly agreeing with the decision, was distressed about the vagueness of "contemporary community standards" and the meaning of "prurient interest." He was also concerned about another question: "Should the literary merit of the product of an author's pen give him carte blanche in case he chooses to venture into forbidden fields?" Unless the legislative bodies spelled out the issues more clearly, Judge Moore said, the courts would "have to continue to struggle with the problem of some vague and ever-retreating boundary line." And then with a sense of humor he added, "Certain it is that if the trend continues unabated, by the time some author writes of Lady Chatterley's granddaughter, Lady Chatterley herself will seem like a prim and puritanical housewife."

The courts seemed to be taking an increasingly lenient position on the obscenity issue.

In 1962 the courts were called upon to decide whether certain magazines aimed at homosexuals were obscene under the federal postal censorship law. The justices of the Supreme Court decided that the magazines would indeed appeal to the "prurient interest" of sexual deviates, "but would not have any interest for sexually normal individuals." Justice Harlan said that the most that could be said of the magazines was that they were "dismally unpleasant, uncouth and tawdry. But this is not enough to make them obscene." Here again, several of the justices questioned basic concepts. Did the Post Office department have the right to censor the mail? Justice Brennan, speaking for three of the justices, thought it did not under the existing circumstances. "Congress has not authorized the Postmaster General to employ any process of his own to close the mails to matter which, in his view, falls within the ban of that [obscenity] section."

All these decisions and opinions of the courts pointed up how very subjective was the question of obscenity. There were the same statutes and the same precedents, and yet there were many conflicting judicial views. What one judge held was not held by another. Or if they concurred in a decision, often it was for very different reasons and interpretations. Then, too, community standards were obviously changing. Indeed, community standards often seemed to be like waves in an ocean, reaching out, then retreating, out and in. There were the waves of purity and pressures, there were the laxity and tolerance of receding waves.

In the early sixties, judging from the then recent judicial decisions, there was an air of relaxation about censorship of the printed word. Thus it was a surprise to many that in 1966 Ralph Ginzburg was sentenced to a five-year prison term under the federal obscenity statute, and that that sentence was upheld by the United States Supreme Court.

Ginzburg was the publisher of *Eros* magazine, a hardcover magazine that contained pictures of nudes, among them those of the glamorous film star, Marilyn Monroe. In the Ginzburg case the Supreme Court justices intimated that a publication that might have been protected under the

First Amendment could be classed as legally obscene because of "prurient" promotional methods and "pandering" advertisements. The justices pointed out that Ginzburg's methods of promoting his magazine—including attempts to mail it from such places as Intercourse, Pennsylvania—were worse than deplorable.

This decision was surprising to those who had followed the actions of the courts, which heretofore had indeed been liberalizing their views on obscenity. But once again perhaps the cognizance of community standards played a part in the decision of the justices.

Since World War II there had been an upsurge of new publishers and new authors. Each year brought forth more and more "daring" books and magazines—materials that were more and more explicit in their details and descriptions of sexual activity. Although it was long past the day of the ginger-whiskered crusader, Anthony Comstock, other pro-censorship groups existed and were driven to action against books and the "smut" magazines.

The Citizens for Decent Literature, which had been founded back in 1956, now had 300 chapters. The Roman Catholic National Office for Decent Literature was busy, as was the Churchmen's Committee for Decent Publications, sponsored by the Protestants. All over the country were signs of the citizens' concern about offensive literature. In California there was a CLEAN (California League Enlisting Action Now) campaign to strengthen the state obscenity law. Connecticut tightened its law. In Philadelphia objectionable magazines were the fuel for a burning attended by the police commissioner and the superintendent of schools. In Boston bright yellow automobile stickers shrieked: Fight Smut. And in the 1964 Republican platform for the Presidential race, enforcement of "legislation, despite Demo-

cratic opposition, to curb the flow through our mails of obscene material which has flourished into a multimillion dol-
lar obscenity racket" was pledged. Indeed, the indications
were that community standards were now raised; a decided
reaction against the growing "permissiveness" in literature
had set in.

The court decision in the Ginzburg case reflected this
sentiment. There was praise for the action from the *New
York Times*, which thought that proper justice had been
given to what it called "an entrepreneur in a disreputable
business who took his chances on the borderline of the law
and lost."

Yet in spite of this public sense of outrage and judicial
warning against obscene literature, the flood of books—including great numbers of paperbacks—containing "filth"
continued unabated during the last years of the decade of
the sixties. Sexual acts were described in detail, abnormal
sexual relationships appeared in book after book. Those who
defended these books which left little to the imagination
claimed they were *literature* which had to be understood if
we were to understand our society. They had "redeeming
social value," which the U.S. Supreme Court had decreed as
necessary for a book to be considered not obscene. But
there were few cases for the Supreme Court to decide. The
public bought this permissive literature eagerly and catapulted many such books onto the best seller lists.

Publishers in the magazine field went as far or further
than book publishers in the late sixties. At many newsstands
across the country, anyone could freely buy magazines that
most intelligent persons classed as pure pornography. The
new publications included those with such frank names as
Screw, Pleasure, and *The New York Review of Sex,* and
those which dealt with homosexuality and lesbianism, in-

cest, bestiality, sadism, and even devil worship. Tamer publications such as *Playboy* could be found for sale in the staidest and most old-fashioned drug stores.

So the sexual explosion continued. Movies such as *I Am Curious (yellow)* showed explicit scenes of love-making; an off-Broadway play, *Hair,* made headlines for nudity; an off-off-Broadway play, *Ché,* featured an ape raping a nun, and what was presumed to be sexual intercourse on stage; and the books celebrating and detailing sexual acts continued to pour off the presses.

What a paradox it was! Voices were raised throughout the country protesting the flood of pornography. Yet, the film *I Am Curious (yellow)* played to crowds who had queued for hours to get into the theater, and broke all attendance records for an "art" film in New York City. The play *Oh! Calcutta!* which had extensive nudity and simulated sex acts onstage, played to packed audiences. The Philip Roth novel, *Portnoy's Complaint,* which boasted "plain talk" about almost every aspect of sex, sold hundreds of thousands of copies at $6.95 each. The public library system of Miami alone had 159 copies of the book for its readers, and still there was a long waiting list.

Obviously a large segment of the American population wanted sexually frank material in the 1960s and 1970s. Yet at the same time that the arts were being inundated by a flood of permissive expressions, written and unwritten, there was also a large segment of the population that wanted to be protected, especially from the pornography that arrived in their mailboxes, unsolicited.

Mail-order pornography had become big business. In 1970, there were reportedly over 200 firms in the country trading in pornography, 75 percent of them in California, sending out offensive advertising circulars to private homes.

A Los Angeles postal inspector said that the distribution of obscene materials through the U.S. mails had "gotten completely out of hand." According to a 1969 report of the U.S. Senate Investigating Committee on Juvenile Delinquency, 75 percent of all this literature eventually fell into the hands of teenagers and younger children, and the mail that came to the home was no exception.

Parents began to object, and the problem received national attention. President Richard M. Nixon, in his message to Congress in May, 1969, said that "American homes are being bombarded with the largest volume of sex-oriented mail in history." He went on: "Most of it is unsolicited, unwanted, and deeply offensive to those who receive it. Mothers and fathers by the tens of thousands have written to the White House and the Congress . . . asking for federal assistance to protect their children against exposure to erotic publications." There were indeed more than 230,000 protests to the Post Office department about unsolicited pornography during the previous year—a number five times as great as that of five years before.

Many officials, responding to such public pressure, began to call, too, for stronger censorship. But they were not to get it from the judiciary. The Supreme Court, still struggling to find a clear definition, had been increasingly liberal in its interpretations of what was obscene. By now criteria used included the prurient interest clause plus the phrase "patently offensive." But even that material which could be classified as the above could not be suppressed unless it had "utterly no redeeming social value." The lower courts had not formulated guidelines that were any clearer.

In April, 1969, the Supreme Court ruled that mere possession of obscene material was not, in itself, illegal. A Georgia man was sentenced by that state to a year in prison because he had obscene films in his home. The Supreme Court overruled the sentence, holding that it constitutionally could not be made a crime to possess obscene films or printed matter in the privacy of a man's home.

Justice Thurgood Marshall, giving the majority opinion of the Supreme Court, said: "The State may no more prohibit mere possession of obscenity on the ground that it may lead to antisocial conduct than it may prohibit possession of chemistry books on the ground that they may lead to the manufacture of homemade spirits." Marshall added that "whatever may be the justification for other statutes regulating obscenity, we do not think they reach into the privacy of one's own home."

Concerning the sending of obscene material through the mails, the Supreme Court agreed to review a Post Office obscenity law that had been in effect only since April, 1968. That law made it possible for any person who received a "pandering advertisement" in the mail to order the Post Office department to forbid further mailings from the sender. If the sender failed to discontinue such mailings, he would face possible prosecution by the Department of Justice.

Under this law one instructor at a midwest university complained to local postal authorities that several firms (including Sears and J. C. Penney) were sending him unwanted "lewd" mail. The local postal official said that the material was not lewd, but the instructor took his case to Washington, claiming that obscenity lay in the eyes of the recipient. He said that since he considered the advertisements for bed sheets, pillows, girdles, and "intimate feminine articles" offensive, he should not have to receive them. The Supreme Court agreed, and the senders were directed to take his name off their mailing lists.

With the Supreme Court still apparently bent toward liberal interpretation, it seemed more likely to many that the curbing of obscenity in the mails could be accomplished through the legislative branch. In 1969 and 1970, a concerted drive for new legislation was initiated. Several bills sponsored by the Nixon Administration were introduced to the House of Representatives judiciary subcommittee, which held hearings on anti-obscenity proposals. By mid-1970, a total of 150 obscenity bills were under study; all of them could be described as attempts to keep "dirty" books, pictures, and advertisements out of the hands of the public, and most especially out of the hands of children. None attempted to liberalize the existing obscenity laws.

The sixties and seventies were a time of unrest, of youthful rebellion, of changing standards of morality, of ever-widening community acceptance of communications materials—movies, TV, theater, art, books, magazines—that would have horrified our grandparents. Citizens wanted to be protected from, and wanted their children to be protected from, those mail-order dealers who made thousands of dollars each year selling erotic literature, hard-core pornography. There was a groping by both judiciary and public for the "right" and constitutional way to solve the problems, but the crucial question remained unanswered. Was it proper that nine men should be the judges and the censors of what Americans might read?

Perhaps, some suggested, we should follow the pattern set in Denmark. In the 1960s that country abolished every legal sanction against pornography for adults. At first there was a rise in sales of such material, then the market fell, and Danish pornographers began complaining. In the year fol-

lowing legalization of written pornography, business de-
creased by 75 percent. Statistics showed that sex crime de-
creased by as much as 34 percent, raising an interesting
point. One of the difficulties that has always existed when
considering the nature of obscenity is that there has never
been established a direct relationship between the reading
of pornography and anti-social behavior. One might judge
from the Danish experiment that more exposure to pornography at least does not cause more crime.

After a pornography fair, "Sex '69," in Copenhagen,
the consensus seemed to be that Danes were fairly tired of
all the fuss about pornography and amazed by the fascina-
tion shown by the foreigners who attended. One Danish
journalist said, "The only thing sensational is the fact that
the fair has drawn more foreign correspondents than
Khrushchev's visit five years ago."

So, for the Danes, the laws were gone, the public could
read and view as it chose, and that public seemed to be
making the wise choices.

CHAPTER 7

Censorship in the Movies

What Do You Say to a Naked Lady? is the name of a movie that features explicit language as well as nudity. It was produced in 1969 by Allen Funt for United Artists, one of the oldest of the Hollywood companies. Funt decided to use the same formula in this film that he had made popular in his television show *Candid Camera.* Average citizens were confronted with an "outrageous" situation—in this case, nudity—and their reactions recorded secretly on film. It is questionable whether the movie which resulted was a new art form for the movies, but it was representative of the upheaval taking place in the industry. As Funt commented: ". . . the sex revolution, or new era of permissiveness, was beginning to happen. It also coincided with the new kind of cinema in which the standard formulas no longer prevailed."

Funt spent $485,000 photographing such ideas as what would happen if a nude girl stepped off an elevator and asked a passing man for directions, or how motorists would react to a nude hitch-hiker. Many moviegoers were also to wonder whether the film would be considered obscene if and when the case came before the Supreme Court. For, just as the final censor of written matter is the Supreme Court of the United States, so is it the final judge for motion pictures.

As the 1970s opened, the nine justices were asked to review a film that had caught the attention of the public. It was the Swedish film *I Am Curious (yellow)*. Released for distribution in late 1968, by order of the U.S. Court of Appeals in New York, the film had since been seen by more than two and a half million Americans in twenty-five states and the District of Columbia. It had been shown to full houses in, among others, New York City, Washington, Philadelphia, San Francisco, Los Angeles, Houston, Atlantic City, San Antonio, Miami Beach, Norfolk, and Boston—and it was banned in Boston. Lawsuits were to be filed against it in thirteen states.

A national weekly newsmagazine called the movie a "dull-but-dirty skin flick." The Maryland attorney general commented: "I don't want my daughter to go out and watch *I Am Curious (yellow)* in an open-air theater and [go out] after that. I want my 16-year-old to have her first sexual experience under circumstances other than that." Dull or dangerous? Obscene or not? Boston banned the film, and a federal court overturned that decision, only to be overturned by the U.S. Supreme Court, which upheld the ban by a 7-1 vote. Justice Douglas, the only dissenter, said he voted as he did because he was against censorship, "not because . . . I relish obscenity."

I Am Curious (yellow) was also banned by Maryland's motion picture censorship board, which precensors all movies to be shown in the state. This decision was upheld by a four to three decision by the state court of appeals. The majority opinion said that the movie taken as a whole "appeals to a prurient interest in sex, and is patently offensive in that it affronts contemporary community standards relating to the description or representation of sexual matters." Judge Thomas B. Finan, writing for the majority, further stated that the movie was "utterly without redeeming social value," and that its overriding theme is "sex per se." The main objective of the picture was, according to Judge Finan, to "purvey shocking and titillating sexual sequences."

As spokesman for the minority, Judge William J. McWilliams said that he did not enjoy the movie, as a matter of fact found it to be "a crashing bore." But he did not believe it was obscene under the standards laid down by the Supreme Court. In explaining why he would have ordered licensing of the movie, he said, "I can not agree with the majority . . . that the film's social and sexual themes were not interwined. . . ."

There it was again—a difference of viewpoints and a difference of interpretations. But probably not under dispute about *I Am Curious (yellow)* and about many movies in the 1970s was the fact that they did, indeed, reflect a change in community standards from a generation before. Jack Valenti, the president of the Motion Picture Association of America, in speaking out about the financial "crisis" of the movie industry today, emphasized that it had as a cause the "radical change in social mores and customs." Just as literature was reflecting a more permissive attitude by the community, so were the movies. What had not changed was the final arbiter, the Supreme Court.

Movies, unlike books, have a relatively short history in the United States. In 1905 came the first newsreel, a fight between Young Griffo and Battling Carnett, and in the same year came the movies. Nickelodeon theaters sprang up everywhere. They charged 5 cents and 10 cents to see little programs of films, no one of which was more than twenty minutes in length. Perhaps because movies were mainly shown in the dark, or because the nickelodeon theaters offered films of dubious quality in often shoddy theaters, community leaders and churchmen became especially aroused about the inherent dangers of the movies to public morality. Because of this, more stringent official censorship was imposed upon motion pictures than on any other artistic medium: that of strict precensorship. Before a film could be shown to the public it had to pass a censor.

The first ordinance of this type empowering a censor to look at motion pictures in advance of their exhibition in order to determine whether they were morally fit for the public to see was adopted by Chicago in 1907, with the police serving as judges. New York City set up its own reviewing board in 1909; many other cities followed this example. The first state censorship board was adopted in Pennsylvania in 1911, then came those of Ohio and Kansas in 1913.

There have been many reasons given why the movie industry tolerated this precensorship, when books, magazines, and newspapers were not subject to such control. Why could not the theater owner or producer first show his film and take his chances as to whether it would be declared obscene or not? Some suggested that it was both because the movie men in Hollywood lacked the courage to protest and also that the Supreme Court was then reluctant to overrule state legislatures and state courts. Whatever the cause, there was no challenge to this system of censorship until 1915. By then the motion picture industry had established an Industry Board of Censors of its own, designed to provide the guidelines for movie production. Movies, however, were still censored before being exhibited.

It was to challenge this precensorship that in 1915 a distributor in Ohio took his case to the Supreme Court, claiming that prior restraint was illegal; that since it could not legally be imposed on newspapers, books, or magazines, it should not be imposed on motion pictures. The Supreme Court disagreed, ruling that the free speech and free press guarantees of the Constitution did not apply to movies. The justices said: ". . . the exhibition of moving pictures is a business pure and simple, originated and conducted for profit, like other spectacles, not to be regarded . . . as part of the press of the country or as organs of public opinion."

Following this decision many states passed censorship laws. Typical of them was that of New York, which provided that a film be licensed "unless such film or a part thereof is obscene, indecent, immoral, inhuman, sacrilegious or is of such character that its exhibition would tend to corrupt morals or incite to crime." A panel of state-employed reviewers would pass on the movies.

By 1922, there were similar censorship bills before the legislature of thirty-two states. Movies had become much bolder after World War I, and at the same time a number of Hollywood stars such as Fatty Arbuckle and Wallace Reid were flaunting the accepted social morality by their personal behavior. Criticism of motion pictures increased.

The industry's leaders realized that something had to be done to still the calls for censorship, so they formed the Motion Picture Producers and Distributors of America (MPPDA), and persuaded Will H. Hays, then Postmaster General of the United States, to accept the position of chairman of the organization. Mr. Hays's job was to improve the public relations of the movie industry and to stave off all censorship attempts. He was successful during the early 1920s but then, in 1926, talking pictures were produced for the first time. With the arrival of sound a new element of realism was added to the movies, and the public clamor against the "sex and violence" in films fairly billowed forth. To appease the critics, Mr. Hays suggested that the MPPDA adopt a "code of morals" to determine what should and what should not appear in pictures. This "Hays code," drawn up by a trade paper publisher and a Roman Catholic priest, was adopted in 1930.

The code did not satisfy the critics, who pointed out that the member producers of the association could accept or could ignore the suggestions of the code as they pleased. Thus, three years later, the National Legion of Decency was established by the Roman Catholic Church to keep an eye on the movies, and the MPPDA felt compelled to make its own code more forceful. It set up a Production Code Administration, which was to read all film scripts of its member producers. It would advise on any undesirable elements in the scripts, and then when the films were finished would review the films. Those films that were acceptable were given a special "seal" and could be released and shown in the theaters of the member companies that had agreed to show only Code-approved films.

With this Code, and the seal, and with the state municipal censorship boards, motion pictures were now in effect getting a close scrutiny. In addition, that powerful private pressure group, the National Legion of Decency, continued to review and classify films according to their moral content and their suitability for showing to audiences. The judgments of this group received wide circulation in the Catholic press, and many Catholics were urged by their churches to follow the recommendations of the Legion.

A panel of voluntary lay persons, mostly women, would view the films and then classify them. A-1 designated movies which were considered morally unobjectionable for general patronage; A-2 were those morally unobjectionable for adults and adolescents; A-3 morally unobjectionable for adults; B morally objectionable in part for all; and C, the lowest of all, meant that a film was totally condemned. A C rating could be disastrous for a theater in a community with a large Catholic population.

Thus for a time there were strong pressures on the motion picture industry to produce nothing that might offend. Then World War II came, and there was, as in literature, more experimentation, more grasping to please a changing society. The old family type films were giving way to what was called a "maturing" of the industry.

In 1948 the major movie companies, in a case brought before the Supreme Court, were ordered to divest themselves of their theater holdings. They were to produce and distribute, but not own the theaters. This may have been an anti-monopolistic action, but the result was that the theater owners, no longer the producers, could show films without the Production Code seal if they so chose. And many so chose. There was after the war a great influx of foreign films, and these, of course, having been produced abroad, carried no seal. Some were divested of certain scenes by state boards of censorship; some were not.

One other interesting point about this Supreme Court case was that for the first time the Court indicated that motion pictures "like newspapers and radio are included in the press whose freedom is guaranteed by the First Amendment." So in the eyes of the Supreme Court justices, movies were no longer just spectacles, but to be considered like other communications as far as their protection by the Constitution was concerned.

This view was to become even clearer several years later when the film *The Miracle* was brought before the Supreme Court.

Made in Italy by Roberto Rossellini, and having Anna Magnani as its star, *The Miracle* told a simple and poignant story. An unmarried peasant woman, who became pregnant by a passing vagrant, believed because of her simple faith that Saint Joseph had caused her to conceive. She was taunted in her village, and endured ordeals at the birth of the child.

The film had been imported by Joseph Burstyn and was at first passed by the New York censor. It opened in one of the city's "art" theaters in December, 1950. Twelve days later the film was ordered stopped by the New York City Commissioner of Licenses who found it "officially and personally blasphemous." The movie was removed, then reinstated. Burstyn took the action of the Commissioner to court and in January of the next year, it was ruled that the Commissioner did not have any authority to stop the showing of a film he did not like.

By this time, the Legion of Decency had condemned the movie, and groups and persons of the Roman Catholic Church, including Francis Cardinal Spellman, had spoken out against it. In addition the New York state censorship board, a three-man committee maintained by the New York Board of Regents, decided to review *The Miracle*. The committee declared the film to be "sacrilegious," and revoked Burstyn's license. Burstyn then sued the Regents, and the case went through the state courts until it finally reached the U.S. Supreme Court in 1952.

Here the justices had interesting points to make. Their decision was to remove the New York ban, stating that ". . . a state may not ban a film on the basis of a censor's conclusion that it is sacrilegious." One of the justices, Stan-

ley Reed, pointed out clearly that the protection of the First
Amendment applied to motion pictures, as well as to newspapers and magazines. He allowed that a state could estab-
lish a system for the licensing of motion pictures, but emphasized that the Supreme Court would have "to examine
the facts of the refusal in each case to determine whether
the principles of the First Amendment have been honored."
Thus he accepted that, as with books, the Supreme Court
would be the final judge in the case of motion pictures, and
that the strict standards of the First Amendment were to be
applied to precensorship of movies.

The justices in this case also pointed up the imprecise-
ness of the word "sacrilegious." By the use of that word
there were "no standards with which to judge the validity of
. . . action which necessarily involves . . . subjective determination."

In the years after *The Miracle* case, the Supreme Court
also labeled words like "immoral," "harmful," and "sexual
immorality" as not capable of a meaning precise enough to
give film makers a clear idea of what was prohibited. Thus
precensorship laws which contained these words were held
to be unconstitutional. But it was not until the next decade
that the Supreme Court would decide on whether precensorship of the movies itself was legal.

The 1950s were a difficult time altogether for the film
industry. The advent and growth of television created a
heavy drop in attendance at movie theaters. Movies had always been the prime source for mass entertainment. They
had had a wide audience: children, young couples on dates,
families—all had enjoyed the outing to the theaters. Now
that mass audience became fascinated with television.
Theatermen bewailed the "lost audience." The number of
theaters declined; the number of movies produced by

American companies declined from 500 or more to 332 in 1952, and 200 in 1961. A flood of foreign films, which were cheaper to make and show, came pouring into the country, so much so that many theaters turned into "art" houses. The names of foreign directors, such as Roberto Rossellini, Vittorio de Sica, Federico Fellini, Michelangelo Antonioni, François Truffaut, Roger Vadim, Ingmar Bergman, became well known.

The American movie makers fought for the attention of the public. In a booklet published by the Motion Picture Association of America (as it was now called), the organization, while chronicling the triumphs of the Code and the caliber of movies produced, took note of the changing community standards. It spoke of the "constantly changing pattern of human behavior" and the fact that "customs, social views and ideas have undergone substantial changes in 25 years." The evidence of changed public attitudes was "public acceptance and even approval of the frankness and the casualness with which certain facets of human behavior, notably those dealing with sex, are discussed and written about. Best selling books, stage plays, paintings, sculpture, even national magazines and daily newspapers, evidence this trend." Defensively the organization claimed that the U.S. motion picture industry "strongly resisted the trend to break down accepted standards. We are not at the head of this parade, nor indeed in the middle of it. We are, in fact, far behind and are proud of it."

Efforts to catch up, however, were soon made. Realizing that there had indeed been an explosion in the arts, in regard to the liberality of what one could read and view, the MPAA in 1956 moderated the restraints of its Production Code. The previous taboos against depicting narcotics traffic, prostitution, abortion, and kidnapping were removed. Ordinary profanity (such as "hell" and "damn") was given the okay when used with discretion. And in general, the Code's administrators were permitted to be more "liberal" in interpreting the other guidelines set down in the Code.

At the same time that the self-regulation of the industry was relaxing, so was the authority of the various state censor boards declining. More and more, through Supreme Court decisions, state boards were being limited to the question of obscenity. After *The Miracle* case, a court of appeals in Ohio declared that that state's censorship statute was illegal. In 1956, the Pennsylvania Supreme Court ruled that the censorship of that state was unconstitutional. Slowly through the years, state after state gave up its censorship board, until in the 1970s only one, that of Maryland, remained.

Was the maintenance of such precensorship by a city or state constitutional? The U.S. Supreme Court had never squarely faced that question. Then, in 1961, before it came *Times Film Corp. vs. Chicago.*

Chicago had an ordinance which stated that before a film could be given a permit to be shown it had to be "produced at the office of the commissioner of police for examination or censorship. . . ." If the picture ". . . is immoral or obscene, or portrays depravity, criminality, or lack of virtue of a class of citizens of any race, color, creed, or religion and exposes them to contempt, derision or obloquy, or tends to produce a breach of the peace or riots, or purports to represent any hanging, lynching, or burning of a human being, it shall be the duty of the commissioner of police to refuse such permit; otherwise it shall be his duty to grant such permit."

Thus the precensor was the Chicago police commis-

sioner. An independent film distributor refused to submit his
movie, *Don Juan*, to the censor. The case went to the U.S.
Supreme Court where the issue became not whether the
film was obscene or not, but whether precensorship of
movies was constitutional. The nine justices split, 5 to 4,
with the majority deciding that precensorship of films was
not unconstitutional. Speaking for the majority, Justice
Clark said, in part, that "Chicago emphasizes here its duty
to protect its people against the dangers of obscenity in the
public exhibition of motion pictures. To this argument the
movie company's only answer is that regardless of the ca-
pacity for, or extent of such an evil, previous restraint cannot be justified. With this we cannot agree. . . ." The justices could not justify stripping a state of "all constitutional
power to prevent, in the most effective fashion, what might
possibly offend the community." Movies, the justices said,
were not "necessarily subject to the precise rules governing
any other particular method of expression."

Thus, for the majority on the court, prior restraint of
movies was legal. What a step-child compared to books and
newspapers!

The minority, however, vehemently protested the decision, and Chief Justice Earl Warren was most eloquent (and
informative) in his dissent. The decision, he said, "presents
a real danger of eventual censorship for every form of communication, be it newspapers, journals, books, magazines,
television, radio or public speeches. . . ." There was, he
continued, "no constitutional principle which permits us to
hold that the communication of ideas through one medium
may be censored while other media are immune. . . ."
There was nothing to "authorize the censorship of one form
of communication and not the others." Justice Warren
spoke of the "vice of censorship through licensing and . . .

the particular evil of previous restraint on the right of free
speech. . . ."

He spoke of the "evils of the censor's basic authority, of
the mischief of the system . . . of the scheme that impedes
all communication by hanging threateningly over creative
thought. . . ."

Then Justice Warren chronicled case after case of censorship in the country. He began first with Chicago. Chicago licensors had banned newsreel films of Chicago policemen shooting at labor pickets. They had ordered the
deletion of a scene showing the birth of a buffalo in Walt
Disney's *Vanishing Prairie*. Before World War II they de-
nied licenses to a number of films showing and criticizing
life in Nazi Germany, including one film by the March of
Time. They refused to give a permit for the film *Anatomy of
a Murder* because they did not like the use of the words
"rape" and "contraceptive." They took out a scene in *Street
With No Name* because they thought that the slapping of a
girl was "too violent." Then Justice Warren pointed to censorship further afield.

He noted that the Memphis censors had banned *The
Southerner,* which was concerned with poverty among ten-
ant farmers, because the film "reflects on the South." In the
same city *Brewster's Millions,* a comedy of many years before, had been forbidden because the radio and film character Rochester, a Negro, was thought to be "too familiar."
Again, the same city banned *Curley* because it showed
white and black children in school together. Atlanta forbade
the showing of *Lost Boundaries,* which told the story of a
black physician and his family who "passed" for white. The
Atlanta censors said the picture would "adversely affect the
peace, morals and good order" in the city.

On and on the chronicle of censorship went: Maryland

restricted a Polish documentary film because it "failed to present a true picture of modern Poland." The same film board had deleted from *Joan of Arc* Joan's exclamation as she stood at the stake: "Oh, God, why hast thou forsaken me?" From *Idiot's Delight* they had removed the sentence: "We, the workers of the world, will take care of that." New York censors banned *Damaged Lives,* which dealt with venereal disease and had the sponsorship of the American Social Hygiene Society. *Professor Mamlock,* which was produced in East Germany and showed the persecution of the Jews by Nazis, was refused a permit by the Providence, Rhode Island, police on the ground that it was "Communistic propaganda." The board in Pennsylvania had banned *Spanish Earth,* a pro-Loyalist documentary on the Spanish Civil War.

Almost any reason seemed good enough for banning. Ohio and Kansas banned newsreels considered pro labor. Chicago banned *The Great Dictator,* Charlie Chaplin's satire on Hitler. New York censors forbade the discussion in movies of pregnancy, venereal disease, birth control, abortion, prostitution, and divorce, among other things.

In Chicago, a police sergeant attached to the censor board said, "Nothing pink or red is allowed . . . anything that would be derogatory to the government—propaganda is ruled out." The head of that censor unit stated that "children should be allowed to see any movie that plays in Chicago. If a picture is objectionable for a child, it is objectionable period."

So Justice Warren in his attack on the majority opinion, wrote of the dangers of censorship, and expressed his opinion that precensorship was much worse than censorship through criminal action taken after the movie had been exhibited. He emphasized the delays in adjudication which could cause much damage. (It took five years for the courts to clear *The Miracle* after the Chicago censor had refused to license it.) He said that with the denial of a license by a pre-censorship board, a film is not shown, perhaps not for years and sometimes never. If the exhibitor of the film did not fight the case in the courts (which he might not want to do because of the time involved and the cost), then his "liberty of speech and press, and the public which benefits from the shielding of that liberty, are in effect, at the mercy of the censor's whim."

Warren warned of the intimidation powers of the pre-censor. The fear of the censor, he said, acted as a substantial deterrent to the creation of new thoughts, and this was especially true of motion pictures, the production of which involved large sums of money. "The censor's sword," Justice Warren wrote, "pierces deeply into the heart of free expression."

Justice William O. Douglas, in agreeing with the minority position, spoke forthrightly about the protection of the First Amendment. It was, he said, "designed to enlarge, not to limit, freedom in literature and in the arts as well as in politics, economics, law, and other fields. Its aim was to unlock all ideas for argument, debate, and dissemination. No more potent force in defeat of that freedom could be designed than censorship. It is a weapon that no minority or majority group, acting throughout government, should be allowed to wield over any of us."

Yet Justice Warren and Justice Douglas *were* in the minority. The majority, as it must, prevailed. Precensorship won out, and is practiced today by some municipalities and the state of Maryland.

During all this period the Motion Picture Association of America was still trying to control its members, and to give guidelines for the content of films produced—this in the face of movies that were becoming each year more frank in sexual matters, and in the face of the increased level of violence in both movies and television. In 1965 a MPAA official spoke of the "two or three" pictures of the previous year that were at the root of the evil (the evil being attempts at legislation designed to control the content of motion pictures). There were also a few theaters which constantly seemed to "brush with the law." There was reference to the "fringe" operator who exhibits "fringe" films that could possibly antagonize a community to the point where the entire industry would be subjected to stringent controls. Films, the organization insisted, which go beyond the customary candor of their community, should not be exhibited.

The same year, Geoffrey M. Shurlock, director of the Production Code Administration of the MPAA, spoke of the value of the Code for the self-regulation of the industry. Under the Code, over 26,500 films had been processed since 1930. In surveying how well the voluntary code system was operating in its objective of helping make Hollywood movies reasonably acceptable, morally, to reasonable people, Shurlock seemed satisfied. The Code, he said, did not "undertake to tell producers what material to choose for their films." All it undertook was to "outline how this material should be treated—in conformity with fundamental standards of morality and within the generally accepted limits of good taste."

Praised that year were such box-office hits as *Mary Poppins, My Fair Lady, Sound of Music, The Ballad of Cat Ballou, Those Magnificent Men in Their Flying Machines,* and *The Greatest Story Ever Told.* Shurlock realized, however, that not all the movies being produced were *Mary Poppins,* and rightly so, he said. When subjects such as adultery,

abortion, sex aberration, dope addiction, and juvenile delinquency were discussed in the magazines and newspapers,
then they rightly could be considered as subjects for the
movies. Years previous there had been taboos against those
subjects, which were written into the Code, but it was not
long before even more touchy and controversial matters
were publicly discussed.

Mr. Shurlock said: ". . . matters such as homosexuality, frigidity and contraception, were being discussed quite
openly and responsibly on television and in family magazines. So we joined the other media and have not abused the
privilege." The MPAA felt that its Code had indeed had an
impact on the producers to raise their standards. In the
1950s and before there had been films dealing with such
subjects as teenage gang rumbles and dope peddling, with
such titillating titles as *High School Hellcats, Gang Girls, Juvenile Jungle, Drag Strip Riot,* and released by respectable
distributors. It was doubtful whether now any responsible
company would think of producing or distributing this type
of "junk."

Yes, the MPAA felt that by its Code it had directed the
treatment of material into films that would win community
acceptance. Yet as the decade of the sixties progressed, the
motion picture industry must have felt that the restrictions
it had placed upon itself by the Code were chafing. According to the MPAA the Code had originally been drafted in
the thirties and "reflected the mores of a depression and
puritanical era." The restraints now seemed "unrealistic
and, indeed, neither reflected nor conformed to the mores
of contemporary society." Cited were magazines that had
"full-page spreads of nudes," newspapers which carried
stories of "wife-swapping and campus cohabitation," women's magazines which sported discussions on all kinds of top-

ics—birth control, adultery, and abortion. It was obvious to the MPAA that "society had changed and motion pictures had remained static." A new code was in order, one that would reflect "contemporary standards as they are portrayed in other media of communication." The motion picture producers wanted to join the theater, books, magazines, and TV in this newly freed society.

So in 1966 a new "Code of Self-Regulation" was adopted by the MPAA. It was, as stated in its declaration of principles, "designed to keep in closer harmony with the mores, the culture, the moral sense, and the expectations of our society." Here again, the script of the film was to be submitted to the Code office, for judgment as to whether it conformed to the Code or not; the completed picture would be reviewed, and given a seal and a certificate number. In addition, the Code's administrators might recommend that the film be labeled as "Suggested for Mature Audiences," if they felt that should be the case.

Among the standards suggested in the Code were the following: "Evil, sin, crime, and wrong-doing shall not be justified; detailed and protracted acts of brutality, cruelty, physical violence, torture and abuse shall not be presented; indecent or undue exposure of the human body shall not be presented; intimate sex scenes violating common standards of decency shall not be portrayed; restraint and care shall be exercised in presentations dealing with sex aberrations; obscene speech, gestures or movements shall not be presented; undue profanity shall not be permitted; religion shall not be demeaned." It was a much briefer code than that formulated in 1956. There was no longer mention of "scenes of passion: (a) these should not be introduced except where they are definitely essential to the plot; (b) lustful and open-mouth kissing, lustful embraces, suggestive posture and gestures are not to be shown; (c) in general, passion should be treated in such a manner as not to stimulate the baser emotions." Gone, too, was point one under the title Costume: "Complete nudity, in fact or in silhouette, is never permitted, nor shall there be any licentious notice by characters in the film of suggested nudity."

The Code was truly streamlined, and gave the motion picture producer wide latitude in what was permitted in films. There was obviously going to be some need for the new appellation "Suggested for Mature Audiences."

CHAPTER 8

The New Movie Ratings

M O S T   O F the motion picture producers had respected the Code and seal, for the seal was a cue to many pressure groups about the suitability of a picture. The Legion of Decency, for example, was very much influenced by the absence of the seal on a movie. Exhibitors knew that boycotts of their theaters might occur, so they tried to avoid the condemned films—those without the seal.

But as movies began to treat with more and more subjects that had once been taboo, various cities, states, and private groups urged a classification system whereby films would be judged according to their suitability. If classification of a picture was done by a government body, it would be enforced by law and any theater owner who permitted a person under the legally established age to see a film classed as not fit for such a person would be subject to prosecution and penalty.

The motion picture industry began to realize that some steps had to be taken if there was not to be classification by law or by government, which they considered to be a "pernicious" form of censorship. The industry also realized that

79

films were now more "mature" and that perhaps vocal parents who were protesting the subject matter in the films their children were seeing were right in that the movies were not always suitable for children.

Thus the motion picture industry, to stave off any lawful classification, and to still the clamor about films unsuitable for children, prepared and adopted a new voluntary code *and* rating system, which went into effect in November, 1968. In announcing the new voluntary film rating plan, the president of the MPAA, Jack Valenti, explained his organization's philosophy. It was against censorship and classification by law. The world, he said, should be as free for film makers "as it is for those who write books, produce television material, publish newspapers and magazines, compose music and create paintings and sculpture." Valenti cautioned, though, that this freedom should be a responsible freedom.

Valenti had a clear view of the different audiences for which motion pictures should be made—not for just "one audience." He said: "There are many audiences and if we seek out the lowest common audience denominator, we will find ourselves making movies that would be . . . inane. We can not allow children to set the boundaries for motion picture creativity, any more than we would allow children to organize our moral apparatus or our national priorities. But we can be concerned about children."

Thus the new Code was established to set apart those pictures that the industry believed parents might not want their children to see. The film rating plan, Valenti said, "assures freedom of the screen, and at the same time gives full information to parents so that children are restricted from certain movies whose theme, content and treatment might be beyond their understanding."

What exactly was this voluntary rating system? All films were classified into one of four categories. G was the rating for films suggested for general audiences; M was for mature audiences (parental discretion advised); R was for restricted—persons under 16 not admitted unless accompanied by parent or adult guardian; and X for persons 16 or under not admitted. This age restriction might be higher in certain areas. Pictures that were rated X would not receive the Code seal. Companies who did not choose to submit their pictures to the Administration were to automatically self-apply the X rating to those pictures.

The MPAA Code Administration could suggest changes to a film maker seeking a higher rating, and there was an appeals board to which the film company could apply if it did not like the rating it was given. Theaters were urged to fully publicize the ratings, and most of them did. They also had to patrol the ranks to see that no young people were admitted to an X film, or to an R film without appropriate escort. Parents seemed to approve of the rating system (thought some felt that the industry did not have the right to forbid their child to see a film, if the parents so desired), and religious groups gave their approbation. But in the 1970s the public was still uncertain as to whether the ratings system would produce better—or baser—pictures. Film makers were now free to make an X movie, without the fear of being accused of corrupting minors. When film makers could be totally adult about the motion pictures, there was a good possibility that many films would be more explicit about sex and violence.

Classifying pictures was difficult, too. There was no attempt to rate quality, but only whether the subject matter was suitable for children. *Funny Girl*, which rated a G, was not "child's fare," but there was nothing inappropriate for children in the movie. *The Charge of the Light Brigade* was one of the first films to receive an M—largely because of the barracks language and the adult nature of its love story. *The Sergeant* was given an R rating, probably because it dealt with a homosexual attraction felt by a tough sergeant for a young private in his company. X films included both those films which were deliberately exploitative of sex, often with "artistic" pretensions but little else, and a number of foreign films which were of serious intent, but showed on the screen scenes unthinkable just a few years before.

The rating system was called industry self-regulation. The MPAA was quick to point out that their Code Administration did not act as a censor. Its role was not to ban, but to inform parents about the motion pictures.

Mr. Valenti, speaking for the MPAA, pointed up a very real continuing problem. "What you and I might believe to be obscene," he told a California audience, "may not be so at all to the educated young. What they consider real and honest, you and I might view as coarse and ugly. Who is right? Each generation in its own turn shapes and forms the mores and the moral sense of the community. Change is endemic in every civilized society."

After fifteen months of the Code Ratings—a "gratifying success," according to the film industry—changes were announced in January, 1970. A survey had shown that there was considerable confusion over the M rating, the rating that signified "for Mature audiences (parental discretion advised)." This category was now dropped, and a GP designation was given. This meant that all ages might view the movies but that parental guidance or discretion was advised. The age limit for viewing films rated R (restricted, without any accompanying parent or legal guardian) was raised from 16 to 17.

Some observers felt that this raise in age limit was to

broaden the scope of films in that category, that perhaps bold but serious films which had been given the X before could now be included in the R.

Jack Valenti, in commenting on the change in ratings, also noted that his original idea of having the X denote a "Leper colony" for films of no artistic quality was not borne out. Two of the most successful and critically acclaimed films of the previous year (1969) had both been X-rated films: *Midnight Cowboy*, which went on to receive the Academy Award for best film, and *Medium Cool*.

The revised ratings now stood thus:

G—all ages admitted

GP—all ages admitted, but parental discretion recommended

R—anyone under 17 must be accompanied by a parent or legal guardian

X—no one under 18 admitted.

The last remaining state censorship board was being challenged as the 1970s opened. It was again in regard to the much publicized film *I Am Curious (yellow)*, which the Maryland state censorship board had banned, with the ban being upheld by the state court of appeals. Now the distributor and the Maryland chapter of the American Civil Liberties Union were asking the U.S. Supreme Court not only to review these decisions, but also to reconsider the constitutionality of the Maryland censorship statute. Prior restraint, said the ACLU, was in contravention of the First Amendment. In addition, they claimed that the Maryland statute suffered "from the fatal defect of vagueness."

According to the statute the board of censors should approve and license such films or views which are moral and proper, and should disapprove such as are obscene (a section of the statute said that the film would be obscene if when considered as a whole "its calculated purpose or dominant effect is substantially to arouse sexual desires, and if the probability of this effect is so great as to outweigh whatever other merits the film may possess") or such as tended, in the judgment of the board, "to debase or corrupt morals or incite to crimes."

The ACLU protested the vagueness of the statute, but also said the Supreme Court should decide whether the rights of the adult citizens of Maryland to "voluntarily view motion pictures is to be subjected to the restraining scrutiny of a board of censors, operating under a vague and overbroad statute."

What exactly was this Maryland board, the last of the precensors? In 1970 the board consisted of three Maryland mothers who were appointed by the governor and confirmed by the state senate. They viewed every film, whether peep show or full-length feature, that an exhibitor wanted to show in Maryland. It cost the state $46,400 in 1969 to maintain the operation in a suite of offices with a small theater in the basement of the State Office Building. Films were screened by at least two members of the board. Exhibitors were charged a fee for the censors' services of $3 per every 1,000 feet of film screened.

In the screening room there were desks on a raised section at the rear, each with a high-intensity lamp. There was an intercom from this room to the projection room. In a nine-month period in 1969 the women viewed 544 films. Some passed, some had changes made in them, suggested by the censors, and some flunked the test. A movie called *Candy Baby* was rejected, changes were made, and on the second try failed again, perhaps due to a semi-nude love scene. *The Best of W.C. Fields* passed, as could be expected. Another film showed sexual intercourse. That failed.

When *I Am Curious (yellow)* was viewed, Maryland's

censors timed what they considered the actual sex scenes at 40 minutes and called them "outrageous." They asked for cuts in the movie and were refused, so it was banned as not coming up to community standards.

Topics that once would have caused a film to be rejected by the board—it has been in existence since 1922—were now accepted without question. Crime and violence were no longer valid criteria for censoring, nor were arson, assault and battery, blackmail, brutality, suicide, drinking, or vulgar language. The Maryland board felt that sexual acts were about the only reason for censorship left.

At the present time, this board is still being challenged. Its life may legally be cut short, or it may continue to be the only such state board.

Thoughtful citizens question censorship of the movies, as they question censorship of literature. Even such a knowledgeable man as Justice Douglas often pondered his role in determining what could be read and viewed. In a dissenting view in a case before the Supreme Court in 1968, he had said:

"Today this Court sits as the nation's board of censors. With all respect, I do not know of any group in the country less qualified first, to know what obscenity is when they see it, and second, to have any considered judgment as to what the deleterious or beneficial impact of a particular publication may be on minds either young or old."

The question of obscenity inevitably involves such subjective judgments. The movies, in their drive to keep up with the other communications media in a relaxed attitude toward sex and violence, *had* caused comment and divergent opinions on the need for control of some kind of the motion pictures. Children were now protected by the X and

R and GP ratings, but was there still unnecessary assault on adults and the community standards by the fare movie producers were offering the public?

Playboy magazine, hardly a conservative publication, in commenting on the movies of 1969, said that pictures "have become by sex possessed and, considering those still in production, the end is nowhere in sight."

Films have always suggested more than meets the eye; but movie makers of the late sixties and early seventies were bolder about what was actually shown on the screen. Some of these films were sincere, some were tawdry. But all critics agreed that never had there been a freer time for the producers and directors. Whether this would lead to the refinement of the movies as an art medium, or whether it would lead to their debasement, remained to be seen. Certainly community standards had changed, and the law—with the Supreme Court as final arbiter—would no doubt take this fact under consideration.

CHAPTER 9

Theater and Art

A N E W   Y O R K judge went downtown to a theater in the last year of the 1960s. He watched a performance of a play, *Ché,* promptly signed a warrant, and the public morals squad hauled off the entire cast of the play and all the production crew they could seize. They were charged with "consentual sodomy, public rudeness and obscenity."

What was this play? Was it an obscenity, an affront to community standards? The play purported to have meaning, that was clear: it was concerned with the last hours of the Cuban revolutionary, Ernesto "Ché" Guevara. Yet, according to *Time* magazine, it was a "squalid series of loveless fornications and related sexual gymnastics, performed in the nude and reminiscent of nothing so much as [a] kind of peep show. . . ."

Earlier the same year six actors and four actresses were arrested at the University of Michigan after they performed in a play in which they had stripped naked. This play, a contemporary version of Euripides' *Bacchae,* was part of the University of Michigan's Creative Arts Festival, and was re-

garded by academic and professional people as worthy of
serious consideration. Perhaps what drew police attention to
the performance was the advance billing, which indicated
that the actors would "kiss and fondle each other from head
to toe."

These two cases pointed up local reactions to the permissiveness that pervaded the arts in the beginning of the
decade of the seventies. The incidents were unusual only
because the theater in general had had for many years almost complete freedom from any form of censorship.

In the very earliest years of drama in the Western
world, the theater was one of the first targets for suppression, mainly because in the days before literacy became
widespread, the theater was *the* form of communication.
The traveling minstrels were the first to arouse the fears of
the Church and the temporal powers. As early as 1605 in
England, if any profanities were uttered on stage, the actors,
playwrights, directors, and producers could be tried by the
courts. Almost a century later the actors who appeared in
Jonson's *Volpone,* Crowne's *Sir Courtly Nice,* and Con-
greve's *Love for Love* were indicted.

England adopted for its theater a special law in 1843,
the Theaters Act, which was and is (it is still essentially the
law governing British plays today) very effective censorship.
This law provides that any theater can be closed by the justice of the peace, if that official believes the theater has
abused its license.

Perhaps even more important, there is precensorship of
the theater in England. Every play must be submitted to the
Lord Chamberlain, the chief censor, in advance of its proposed performance. This official has very wide powers. If he
considers the prohibition of the play to be "fitting for the
preservation of good manners, decorum, or public peace,"

he will forbid the showing of the play. Thus, from the time
of the passage of the Theaters Act until the present, many
plays, including Tennessee Williams's *The Rose Tattoo* and
Arthur Miller's *View from the Bridge,* have not been performed in England, except in "private clubs," which do not
come under the jurisdiction of the government.

Surprisingly, since the United States patterned so much
of its laws concerning judgments on books after those of
England, this country did not adopt a similar precensorship
for the theater. There were always some organizations or individuals, however, who opposed various forms of drama.
Back in the days of Anthony Comstock, the New York Society for the Suppression of Vice opposed the "degrading
shows" at the Chicago World's Fair in 1893. The same society in 1931 prided itself on being active against "obscene
Christmas cards," and "burlesque shows." In 1939, when
celebrating its 66th year, the Society forced the withdrawal
of "girl shows" at the New York World's Fair, and even as
late as 1942 they were investigating the "indecent nature of
a floor show in a downtown night resort." But there were
not very many direct efforts to censor drama in the theaters.
There was, of course, Comstock's effort to close down
George Bernard Shaw's *Mrs. Warren's Profession,* but that
came to naught, since the court ruled that the play did not
fall within the scope of the New York state obscenity law.

That was in 1905. By 1927, when the subject of homosexuality was beginning to raise its head in public, another
play attracted much attention: Edouard Bourdet's *The Cap-
tive,* which was a lesbian-oriented drama. The discussion of,
and the attention to, this play caused the New York legislature to act. A state law was passed stipulating that no performances would be permitted of any drama that dealt with
sexual perversion. Any theater owner who permitted such a

play to be shown could lose his license and the theater could be closed.

But through the years it was mainly the pressure groups who sought to ban plays which they felt were objectionable, and often the criterion was not obscenity or indelicacy, but whether the play's material or treatment of it offended various religious or minority groups. Jewish organizations, for example, objected to the presentation of Shakespeare's *Merchant of Venice* on the basis that one of its characters, Shylock, was not a very pleasant Jew. To exhibit this character, according to the protesters, was to defame Jewish people.

Some black organizations protested and caused to be temporarily banned a musical version of *Uncle Tom's Cabin*. The groups claimed that the play "refreshed memories that tend to portray only the weaknesses of a racial minority," and that it ridiculed "peoples who in the early days of our country were unfortunately subjected to exposures that today would be considered atrocious."

Even official bodies sought to censor some theater. In Chicago, Jean Paul Sartre's *The Respectful Prostitute* was banned. Although the play had run for many months in New York, a police captain of the Chicago Crime Prevention Bureau claimed that the play was likely to provoke interracial troubles.

There have been many isolated cases of protests about the theater, but as with movies, the medium has become freer and freer to make use of the new permissiveness of community standards. A look at some of the plays performed in the 1970s shows that there is indeed a wider range of what will be tolerated on stage today than ever before.

Some like *Ché*, though, had their troubles with the authorities and the courts. As the eight defendants from that play faced a total of 54 charges, which included lewdness and obscenity in connection with their parts in the production, defenders of such plays spoke about their own rights and the public's rights and the artists' rights to express themselves freely. In this discussion one social commentator noted that the usual argument against censorship was that freedom of expression protects the public. Yet he also warned that that argument "begins to lose its force unless we also take seriously the right of the public to be protected against nonconsentual assaults on its sensibilities."

The fact seemed to be that in the beginning of the 1970s the public wanted to expose itself to the various free expressions on the stage, judged by the large attendance at such well-publicized performances. *Hair,* one of the first dramas to cause talk because it contained one scene which involved nudity, had won world-wide fame. Billed as "America's tribal love-rock musical," it had successful productions in Chicago, Los Angeles, and San Francisco. It had also played to enthusiastic audiences in England, France, Germany, Yugoslavia, Australia, and Japan.

In *Oh! Calcutta!* the five men and the five women in the play danced and pranced about naked for about half the show. *Playboy* magazine noted that they "fondle, mock-fornicate, group-grope and fool around a lot." The editors felt that the play's contribution to theater was its "unpretentious, unkinky presentation of nudity." Police in Los Angeles thought differently. They raided the play twice, and after five weeks in that city, the play closed.

These were the glaring examples of how the theater had embraced the new freedom in the arts; to be sure cities all over the country were presenting more traditional, or less sexually spectacular productions. But it was obvious that the theater, which had been relatively free from censorship in the past, was retaining that freedom and even expanding on it.

Art, of course, had with rare exceptions been little touched by the brush of the censor. However, as noted previously, it was pictorial art that drew the first censorship laws, when Congress passed the 1842 customs law. It was enacted that "the importation of all indecent and obscene prints, paintings, lithographs, engravings, and transparencies is hereby prohibited." These, if found by the customs, would be seized and destroyed. In 1857 the law was changed so that the category of items that could be seized was enlarged. "Images and figures" were included, as were "indecent daguerreotypes and photographs." It is thought that these original laws were framed for fear of the French postcards that had titillated many American travelers.

A British member of Parliament that same year chided the U.S. Customs officials for their attitude on the obscene. He reported that an American traveler, returning home from Italy, had brought a copy of *Museo Barbonica Reale*— a book costing between $150 and $200, and which described the figures, statues, and paintings of the Royal Museum of Naples. The work was deemed obscene and destroyed by the collector of the customs at New York, yet a copy of the same book was in the library of the Parliament.

There was through the years censorship of art, largely through the customs law, or by pressure groups in communities, but generally art enjoyed the same freedom as the theater. However, in Comstock's law of 1873, pictorial matter was included in the ban against mailing obscene material, and a number of publications which featured art work were prosecuted under this law.

Museums had always had objects which were suspect to the pure-minded. (Note the use of fig leaves in the 1800s.) Comstock had carted off some loads of "anatomical filthiness" from museums. Private citizens and organizations had often protested about various art works, but as community standards became more enlightened (or permissive) there were few outcries that reached the attention of the public.

By the end of the decade of the sixties, however, it was noticeable that the freedom of sexual expression had spread into the art field. Art galleries and museums faced an aroused public, or even official action in some cases. In Los Angeles, city councilmen sought—in vain—to close a County Museum of Art show, which included a painting they felt was improper. It was a graphic three-dimensional representation of a young boy with his date in the back seat of an old Dodge, with high sexual interest. The police in the same city tried to close another show by 43 artists, which included works depicting larger than life sexual organs.

It was not always sexual matters that aroused disgust and ire. Washington, D.C.'s Corcoran Gallery of Art sponsored a show which consisted of original drawings for comic strips published in the underground press. Many of these had heavy accents on drugs, violence, and racism, in addition to sex. Here the director, Walter Hopps, took a position that he hoped would be satisfactory to the public. "Rather than censor the artists," he said, "we've decided to warn our visitors. If their sense of decorum is offended by four-letter words or outrageous drawings, they ought to proceed at their own risk."

Perhaps the case which caused the most public discussion was that involving an exhibition of erotic art which had been shown, with considerable acclaim, in museums in Sweden, Denmark, and Germany. Of the 1200 pieces (among them works by Rembrandt, Picasso, and Chagall) in that collection, ten were selected to be sent to the United States as a test because the customs bureau had refused to guarantee that the paintings would be returned to their owners if they were deemed obscene by the courts. The paintings were seized by the U.S. Customs officials in 1969, and the Department of Justice claimed that they were "obscene" and sought the authority to keep the rest of the collection from entering the country. The lawyer defending the case said that the works (by George Grosz, Hans Belmar, and Karel Appel, and several anonymous artists from Japan, China, and India) were no more salacious than "the lyrics of Catullus or Donne or the nudes of Michelangelo or Rubens."

Were the erotic paintings obscene? The lawyer claimed they were "unquestionably . . . of serious artistic intent and genuine . . . merit." When the collection, valued at more than $1 million, was shown for the first time in Sweden, a conservative Swedish newspaper had published detailed pictures and commented: "On the whole, far more harmless than our ordinary men's magazines."

But here again, the fate of the ten seized paintings was decided in the courts. The government's challenge was unsuccessful. And here again, subjective judgments as to the meaning of obscene came into play. That is the trouble with cultural censorship and always will be.

CHAPTER 10

Television and Radio

T W O   A L L I E D   media which have never been subjected to official censorship are radio and television. In the early 1920s when commercial radio broadcasting became a burgeoning industry, the federal government was called upon to license and regulate their technical operations. This was to avoid traffic jams in a limited amount of air space for all the radio stations that wished to operate. In 1927, Congress passed a Radio Act establishing the Federal Radio Commission which was empowered to grant broadcast licenses. This group was superseded in 1934 by the Federal Communications Commission, which was given authority to regulate all interstate and foreign communication by wire and radio, including telegraph, telephone and broadcast, and more recently, television.

The FCC is empowered to tell station owners the frequencies they must use, the extent of their broadcast power, the areas they must cover, and the specific hours they can operate. It has no power, however, to restrict the broadcaster as to the content of his programs. The 1934 act establishing the Commission clearly stated that there would be "no regulation or condition . . . promulgated or fixed by the Commission which shall interfere with the right of free speech."

The act also established that the airwaves belonged to the people, whose property rights in them the federal government was required to protect. Licenses, therefore, were to be granted to those ostensibly best fitted to serve "in the public interest, convenience or necessity." As airwaves are limited, and as licenses once granted must be renewed periodically (at present every three years), the Commission does have, then, potentially, great power. However, the FCC has seldom used it, and has with very rare exceptions always extended licenses as a matter of course.

Television, which got its first real public demonstration at the New York World's Fair in 1939, came under the FCC when the Commission authorized the first commercial television operation on September 1, 1940. World War II halted the construction of new stations and the manufacture of receivers, but after the war there was a rush of stations applying for licenses to operate. The Commission grants licenses to radio and television owners if they prove their financial and technical ability to build and maintain a broadcast station. At the time of application the owners must also make a declaration of the kind of program schedule they intend to present in their assigned community or area. At the end of three years, when the license is up for renewal, the Commission reviews the station's programming to see how it has measured up to what was originally proposed.

The only current regulation of radio and television content is self-regulation. The National Association of Broadcasters, a non-profit organization which was formed in 1922, has both a voluntary radio and a voluntary television code.

These codes set standards for the broadcasters—standards about what is right, proper, and in good taste. There is a NAB Code Authority headquarters in Washington, D.C., which counsels and aids broadcasters, but theoretically the director of the Authority does not act as a censor. It is up to the individual broadcasters to decide what shall or shall not be aired on radio or TV. The Television and Radio Codes are each supervised by a board.

The Radio Code was first drawn up in 1937, and had gone through fifteen revisions by 1970. It contains standards for news, controversial public issues, community responsibility, political broadcasts, religion, responsibility toward children, and other areas. It has standards for radio advertising, and also general guidelines, such as those forbidding profanity, obscenity, smut, and vulgarity.

The Television Code, first adopted in March, 1952, is similar, setting forth optimum goals and responsibilities and general standards. Here again are included interdictions on profanity and obscenity, any words derisive of any race, color, creed, etc., any attacks on religion. On the positive side there are pointers that respect be maintained for the sanctity of marriage and the value of the home. Illicit sex relations are not to be treated as commendable. Narcotics addiction should not be presented except as a vicious habit, and important in current discussions about violence on television, "the detailed presentation of brutality or physical agony by sight or by sound are not permissible."

The adherence to these Codes is voluntary. Stockton Helffrich, the director of the NAB Code Authority, however, has called himself a "reluctant censor." In an interview in the August 23, 1969 *TV Guide*, Helffrich spelled out his job: to solicit the voluntary compliance with the Code. Here again, however, community standards come into play,

for Helffrich feels that his main duty is to keep TV's mores
abreast of the permissiveness of the age without running
counter to the puritan-minded among the television viewers.

"Society," he said, "is tolerating greater candor, and
the Code endeavors to respond to the sentiments of broadcasters and viewers alike. . . . Big changes are occurring in
our society. This is, after all, the era of the Pill and the
Bomb and such things affect our attitudes. . . . We do try to
react to what the public feels is quote right unquote. . . .
Young people today, for instance, are more honest and candid in their approach to sex." Thus Helffrich felt that the
network programming was reflecting this increased candor,
and that the networks were responding "to a greater open-
ness on the part of the audience, while not pressing it too
far." He did feel that the NAB, which monitors many of the
programs, was a factor in the networks' efforts to cut back
on violence on TV, which had during the late sixties become
more and more a topic of discussion.

The National Commission on Violence reported in
1969 that television programs were contributing to violence
in America. Very strongly they stated that with its "constant
portrayal of violence," television was "pandering to a public
preoccupation with violence that television itself has helped
to create." In this, its fourth report on violence in the
United States, the Commission said that "violence on television encourages violent forms of behavior and fosters moral
and social values about violence in daily life which are unacceptable in a civilized society."

The Commission deplored the fact that ". . . we daily
permit our children during their formative years to enter a
world of police interrogations, of gangsters beating enemies,
of spies performing fatal brain surgery and of routine dem-

onstrations of all kinds of killing and maiming." The Commission felt that the standards as set forth in the NAB Code were inadequate, and failed to get to the heart of the problem of violence on TV.

The uproar about violence on television was of significance to the industry, for there was Congressional interest in greater regulation of television. Senator John Pastore called upon the networks and independent broadcasters to root out violence in news and entertainment and "clean up the dirt," and he proposed rigorous control of the networks by the NAB Code Authority, which he felt had not been active in policing its own ranks. Pastore proposed that networks submit their programs to the Code Authority *before* they went on the air, in other words, that there be precensorship of television. It will be interesting to see if Congress takes any positive action along the lines of this proposal.

The matter of sex in television was brought to the public's attention when Dean Burch, chairman of the FCC, stated that some steps had to be taken by the Commission in an effort to keep movies that dealt openly with sex off the home television screens. It has always been rather ironic that while movies may be precensored in some municipalities and in the state of Maryland, such movies could conceivably be shown there on TV that reached into a saloon, a home, or a church, due to the fact that there is currently no precensorship of television.

Burch's concern was that if a television station wanted to show the much discussed *I Am Curious (yellow)*, which was banned in Boston and in Maryland, the FCC could do nothing to prevent the viewing of that film on television. That the FCC might possibly do something about this situation was indicated by Burch, a relatively new chairman of the FCC, when he said he thought the strict definitions of what is obscene set down by the Supreme Court for books, movies, and art, was "an entirely different standard to something that comes into the home."

Burch felt that films became objectionable when shown on TV where, for example, a five-year-old might see them. He reasoned that such a five-year-old would not be affected by *Lady Chatterley's Lover* because he could not read, nor would he be permitted into a theater to see *I Am Curious (yellow)*. He could, however, easily turn on the TV. Burch called for the FCC to set up guidelines for movies on TV, but as of this writing, none have been adopted.

Radio has not come into the limelight as much as television recently over the contents of its programs, but critics spoke out sharply against much of its material at a 1969 conference in Atlanta, Georgia. During these sessions of the Radio Program Conference, some 900 people from the radio and recording industry met to talk about what to put on the air and how. Of course, the voluntary Radio Code was to be followed, but some unusual comments were made on how well radio was performing its functions.

One newspaper commentator was shocked at what the members at this conference revealed about their trade and themselves. Most of those attending were from stations with a few employees, "a couple of deejays or used car salesmen" reading the news. This type of station is in the majority, according to reports, stations that the industry calls "rockers," "top-40," "MOR" (Middle of the Road), "C&W" (Country and Western), and "R&W" (Rhythm and Blues).

One spokesman, a news director from a Texas station, who took part in a panel, was forthright in speaking of his station's appeal and aims. It appeals to "a guy in a bar. . . . We know our audience," he said. "We know exactly who they are and they associate with me because I and the other newsmen there, we speak for them, we say what they want to hear and it sells." This news director went on to say that his main drawing card was sensationalism, that death could be fun, it could be sold. "When we get the television station on the air and the six o'clock news features the in-color showing of an autopsy, they'll all be tuned in to us."

Some of the other radio representatives at this conference were aghast at hearing such sentiments, but unfortunately it has been true that many of the radio and TV station owners have shown great irresponsibility to their medium and the public, which, supposedly, is the owner of the airwaves these stations exploit. One radio general manager sadly commented: ". . . we communicate the fact that we are phony, money-grubbing, material acquisitive shucks. . . ." If the general public finally receives that same impression there may be greater consideration given to radio and TV program content than there is at the present time.

CHAPTER 11

Censorship by Pressure

I T   I S most ironic that while the courts were restricting the censorship powers of the government as far as obscenity in the media was concerned, private vigilantes were alarmingly on the increase. None of them had the flair and ebullience of Anthony Comstock, but they did have the same urge to protect everyone's morals.

The pressure was as varied as that of the little old lady in the Midwest who took a paperback book off a bookstore counter to save others from being corrupted, to that of organized groups who gave lists of indecent literature to the police department, and then attempted to coerce the booksellers. But add example after example of such pressure to impose censorship, attempted and completed, which occurred throughout the country and the result was a sizeable effort to channel what we read, and hear, and see.

Pressure by private parties and individuals is certainly not a new phenomenon, nor did it begin with Comstock. Back in 1806 the Boston *Ladies' Visitor* in its very first issue declared that the magazine would be "closed against politics and obscenity" and against "everything which might cause the crimson fluid to stain the cheek of unaffected modesty." A few years earlier the principal commencement address at Harvard had been concerned with the indecencies and moral dangers of novel reading.

Novel reading—and protests against it—increased enormously with the passage of the years. Even before World War II cheap production facilitated the serious emergence of paperbacks. Here now was mass production for mass distribution. There were novels aplenty for readers —and for self-appointed censors. And especially because the soft-cover books were inexpensive, and thus within the reach of youth, attention was drawn to their content. Many of the "good" books were now more available to the masses, but so, too, were a great number of "trash" books, with lurid covers which often had little to do with the content.

Citizens became aroused at what they saw in the candy stores, and on the newsstands. Often censorial action came about because of "public-spirited" individuals. Such was the case in Georgia when the Reverend James Pickett Wesberry, chairman of the Georgia State Literature Committee, reported the alarm of such citizens at the "display of salacious material freely accessible to the young and impressionable at prices easily accommodated by young allowances. . . ."

The original members of this commission were a Baptist clergyman and "two of the noblest and finest laymen God ever made." They were empowered to investigate "all sales of literature which they have reason to suspect is detrimental to the morals of the citizens of this State." The commission was to hold hearings, make findings and to "prohibit the distribution of any literature they find to be obscene." If they prohibited a book, and the sales continued, they were to recommend prosecution. There were no special qualifications for the commission members; they were merely to be Georgians "of the highest moral character." And here was the rub, as it was to be with so many private censorship groups.

Such censors are of necessity amateurs, frequently not representative of the standards of a given community, and more often than not possessing little knowledge of the law. There was, for example, the old lady in a Minnesota city responsible for the removal of over 300 books who was described by an admirer as a "white-haired grandmother, who manages a small grocery store. She looks on the task of censorship as a 'matter of salvation of souls.'"

The difficulty is that the views of such individuals are not just expressed as their own, and then forgotten. These individuals put pressure either upon public officials to take action against what they feel is objectionable, or they make efforts themselves to intimidate the sellers into "voluntary cooperation" with the "decent citizens of the community." Sometimes reliance is put upon the police to "persuade" shop-owners to eliminate materials that the private censors deem unsuitable, but more often there is the use of awards to those stores that voluntarily remove certain material from sale, or the threat of a boycott if they do not.

There are examples of private pressure from all over the country. An indignant mother protested to the Secretary of State of Illinois that her teenage daughter had been "polluted" by a book. As a result that official had drawn up a list of offensive books, which he felt should be removed from the public libraries throughout the state. The list grew to 500 titles, and over 6,000 library books were withdrawn before someone realized the scheme was both unwieldy and ridiculous.

A "Minute Woman" started trouble in a large south-western city by claiming that a great number of books in the public library were "Communist connected." As a result of her complaint the city manager of that city recommended that those books be burned. (They included an edition of *Moby Dick.*)

All over the country, individuals, religious groups, citizens' committees, parent-association committees, and local branches of organizations like the American Legion act as self-styled censors. Their objections to any of the media are not made solely on grounds of indecency, but often because certain material runs counter to their own beliefs.

Witness the following: *The Nation* was banned from the New York City public schools because the magazine had carried articles criticizing some activities of the Roman Catholic Church. In Philadelphia, a Roman Catholic priest objected to a movie, and prevented its exhibition by threatening that his parishioners would boycott not only that film, if shown, but all films shown at the particular theater. By protesting its importation, Jewish organizations prevented for two years the showing of the English film version of *Oliver Twist* because they did not like the characterization of Fagin.

Branches of the National Association for the Advancement of Colored People made attempts to prevent the showing of *The Birth of a Nation,* and to stop touring companies of *Uncle Tom's Cabin.* Attempts were made to keep the television programs *Beulah* and *Amos and Andy* off the air, by economic boycott. The American Legion in Illinois tried to prevent performances of *Death of a Salesman,* because the author, Arthur Miller, was called subversive.

When the groups acting as censors have an official or semi-official status, they can, of course, more directly enforce their viewpoints.

In Boston a board composed of the mayor, the police

commissioner, and a member of the city art commission held censorship powers over theater productions. If a majority of this board deemed a play violated "public morality or decency," the theater owner risked a revocation of his license if he sponsored the play. To avoid economic difficulties, the theater owners voluntarily subjected themselves to the judgment of a censor appointed by the mayor. Needless to say the censor was not an expert in either theater or literature.

Police in various cities often are eager to be censors, and conduct campaigns against so-called obscenity. In Cleveland, in one such drive, booksellers were intimidated into withdrawing from sale Sigmund Freud's *General Introduction to Psychoanalysis* "because it had a chapter on sex." *The Golden Ass* by Lucius Apuleius was banned because "the title might be offensive."

One of the most notorious of the police censorships was that in Detroit. In 1951 what was called the Detroit Line came into being. Up to that point Inspector Herbert W. Case of the police license and censor bureau could not act until a book went on sale. But now he decided to censor books at the source, by telling the distributor what not to distribute. He compiled an obscenity list, which was reviewed each month. It became known as the Detroit Line, since many other self-appointed censors in other towns used the list in their own communities. Case's policy was to "skim off the filth, so to speak, at the top," by seeing that the books were not offered for sale.

To determine the objectionable books, Case had twelve policemen working day and night reading books; in an average year they might spend 750 hours of overtime doing such reading. Among those books banned by the Detroit Line were Ellis's *Psychology of Sex*, John Dos Passos's *1919*, J. D.

Salinger's *The Catcher in the Rye*, Ernest Hemingway's *Across the River and into the Trees*, Hans Christian Andersen's *Fairy Tales*, James Jones's *From Here to Eternity*, and Leon Uris's *Battle Cry*.

Perhaps two of the most effective pressure groups (though they did not like to be called by that title) were the National Legion of Decency and the National Office for Decent Literature. The Legion of Decency, as noted earlier in the chapter on movies, was created in 1933 by the Catholic bishops of the United States at an annual meeting. The Legion was to arouse Catholic opinion against the low moral tone of some films. It devised its system of classification, where movies, after review by members of the Legion, were given a rating based on the morality of the movie. Then Catholics were to follow the listing of the Legion and stay away from pictures that were, in some degree, condemned. It was admittedly censorship by boycott. For many years this Legion of Decency had an important influence, for many producers did not want to lose such a widespread audience. (The Legion also was sometimes asked by producers for an opinion on a script in progress and sometimes changes were made in the film as a result.)

While all the communities were alerted to the Legion ratings, by pastoral letter, sermons, and so on, some local bishops went even further. The Bishop of Albany, New York, for example, in 1957, forbade Catholics to attend for a period of six months a theater that had shown the C-rated film, *Baby Doll.* And New York's Cardinal Spellman issued a strong condemnation of the same film, urging "all decent-minded and patriotic citizens" to join in the Catholic protest against the movie. The Legion is now called the National Catholic Office for Motion Pictures, having changed its name in 1966.

The National Office for Decent Literature was established by the Catholic bishops of the United States in 1938.
According to its code, it was "to safeguard the moral and
spiritual ideals of youth" through a program designed to
"remove objectionable comic books, magazines and pocket-
size books from places of distribution accessible to youth."
Reviewers evaluated the above mentioned, and if any were
found objectionable they were placed on a list which was
checked monthly. Parish committees were urged to visit,
every two weeks, various establishments, including newsstands that sold comic books, magazines and pocket-size
books, and give the bookseller a copy of the NODL list, and
if the committee members found any objectionable titles,
they were to "courteously ask that they be removed from
sale." If the manager refused, the members would "leave si-
lently and report the refusal to their pastor, who can determine future action." Further, stores that cooperated were to
be "mentioned from the pulpit or listed in the parish publication with a word of commendation."

The NODL lists themselves were often used by non-
Catholics to coerce. In Youngstown, Ohio, in 1953, the chief
of police ordered news dealers to clear their stands of material disapproved of by the NODL, and threatened penalties
if the dealers failed to comply. This case did go to the
courts, and it was decided that the officer had exceeded his
authority, and that books could be banned from distribution
only after they were found to violate the state obscenity
laws. Similar cases occurred through the country, in spite of
the NODL denial that it had ever recommended or encouraged any arbitrary coercive police action.

In all fairness to the NODL, it did aspire to appeal to
all "moral forces to combat the plague of indecent literature," not just Catholics. However, it came under attack by

the American Civil Liberties Union, not because it wanted to warn Catholics and the general public about certain writings, but because of its extended actions. The ACLU protested the calls upon the booksellers asking that condemned titles not be offered for sale and the threats to non-complying booksellers that they would be boycotted. The ACLU objected to the fact that "the judgment of a particular group is being imposed upon the freedom of choice of the whole community," and accused the NODL of attempting to act as a private morals-police force. In a statement, the ACLU went on to say: "The novel which may be thought by a committee of Catholic mothers to be unsuitable for a Roman Catholic adolescent is thus made unavailable to the non-Catholic. It is plainly necessary to challenge the NODL as keeper, by self-election, of the conscience of the whole country."

A partial list of NODL banned books included those by Pulitzer Prize winners William Faulkner (*Sanctuary; Soldiers' Pay*) and Ernest Hemingway (*To Have and Have Not*). Other authors listed were John Masters, Alberto Moravia, John O'Hara, J.D. Salinger, William Styron, Gore Vidal, James M. Cain, Vicki Baum, John Dos Passos, Kathleen Winsor, Will Oursler, and Émile Zola (for *Nana*).

Concern for young people has played a part in other attempts at censorship in our schools and libraries. The subject of textbooks has always been a thorny one, due to pressure brought by various individuals or groups. One-time president of the American Textbook Publishers Institute, William E. Spaulding, bemoaned irresponsible criticism of textbooks, and the resulting defamation of textbook character merely by suspicion. In some areas textbook selection is entrusted to professional advisors of the highest order, while in other areas, persons less competent are given the job.

And their decisions are important, for publishers want a textbook that is acceptable in all areas; if a textbook is taboo in one section of the country, it is likely that suspicion will be cast upon it in another.

Naturally, it was not obscenity that bothered critics of the books used by our school children. Most often it was the charge of "un-American" or "subversive." The height of this type of criticism was reached in the years after World War II.

Textbooks which had been used for years came under fire as superpatriots began their sleuthing. Dr. Benjamin Fine, long-time education editor of the *New York Times*, reported on a few of them. *American Government* by Frank Magruder had been used as a history text for over thirty years. Then came a review of the book in *The Educational Reviewer*, published by the Committee on Education of the Conference of American Small Business Organizations. The book, according to the reviewer, had socialistic and Communistic overtones. As a result, state after state cancelled use of the book. The state of Georgia and the city of Houston, Texas, banned it outright. There was dissension about it in Council Bluffs, Iowa, Washington, D.C., Jackson, Michigan, Trumbull County, Ohio, and New Haven, Connecticut. Some of the communities fought against the criticism and for the book. A New Haven committee cleared the book for use. Council Bluffs decided to keep it, and so did Trumbull County. The Florida department of education decided that the book was "objective, accurate, and fair." But, to be sure, the book had been maligned by the critics, and the public would remember.

Another case involved a book on basic economics written by four Rutgers University professors. The instigator of criticism was the writer of an anonymous letter to the Phoenix, Arizona, *Gazette*, demanding that the book be dropped from Phoenix College. The American Legion took up the cause; a committee of the local chapter examined the book and found that it was "socialistically and communistically inclined." It urged that the book be dropped. Although the educators involved defended the book, which had been adopted by forty colleges and universities, it had now been tarred with the brush of suspicion.

A women's civic group in Sapulpa, Oklahoma, picked out a number of books from that town's high school library, and tossed them into a blazing fire. The books were "bad" because they "used improper language in the presentation of ideas."

And so the fire of irresponsible criticism spread. As teachers and superintendents were loath, many times, to jump into the fray, it was often the pressures of individuals and groups that actually controlled what children could read in the schools.

What was happening in the schools was also happening to many of the public libraries throughout the country. The Boston Public Library, the oldest tax-supported library in the United States, came under severe attack in 1952. The newspaper, the Boston *Post*, led the attack, starting at the time it began serialization of Senator Joseph McCarthy's book *McCarthyism and the Fight for America*. The *Post* first complained that the book was not in the Boston Public Library (although it noted that the book had been ordered and would soon be available to the public). Then it charged that the library had available, on request, files of the *New World Review*, *Pravda*, and *Izvestia*; also that it had a copy of Karl Marx's *Communist Manifesto* in a lobby display arranged by the Great Books Foundation; and further that in its reference collection it had Vishinsky's *Law of the Soviet State* and "thousands of other Communist publications."

The library did not deny any of the charges, for they

were, indeed, true. But the library director was hasty to point out that the inclusion of this material in the library was a positive planned policy: "It is essential that information on all aspects of political, international, and other questions be available for information purposes in order that citizens of Boston may be informed about the friends and enemies of their country."

Nevertheless, the attack on the library continued. The Boston *Post* said: "We believe that pro-Soviet literature should be suppressed in our public libraries. . . ." Two local American Legion commanders, the president of the city council and one councilman joined in criticism of the library.

But in the city, other newspapers came to the defense of the library and finally the library trustees (by a three to two vote) passed a resolution declaring that material presenting all points of view concerning the problems and issues of our times, international, national, and local, should be made available to the public. They declared that the library authorities had no right to prescribe what the public was and was not to read.

The next year, in San Antonio, Texas, controversy over the library system there became quite heated. An organization of the San Antonio Minute Women presented to the city council a list of 600 books, allegedly by Communist sympathizers, with the recommendation that those books "be stamped on the inside cover with a red stamp, large enough to be seen immediately, showing that the author has Communist front affiliations, and the number of the citations." The mayor of the city, whose wife was a Minute Woman, urged that this proposal be adopted. The acting city manager urged even stronger action—that the books on the list be burned.

And what were these books? They included books of poetry and folk songs, books on sculpture, the mentally ill, alcoholics, child care, architecture, and mystery novels. They also included Einstein's *Theory of Relativity*, Thomas Mann's *Joseph in Egypt* and *The Magic Mountain*, Dorothy Canfield Fisher's *Fable for Parents*, and Norbert Wiener's *Cybernetics*.

San Antonio's chief librarian admitted that the library had books on Communism, as well as books by alleged or known Communists, but she defended this by stating that the books were chosen so that the reader might learn all that should be known about Communists. "After all," she said, "you cannot remain ignorant about a thing and fight it."

The attack, and the defense, by a great number of civic groups who had organized to support the library's position, continued for some time, but eventually the library board adopted—but by a bare majority—the American Library Association's "Bill of Rights" as its official policy of book selection. This Bill of Rights, which was first adopted by the ALA in 1948, stated that in no case "should any book be excluded because of the race or nationality, or the political or religious views of the writer." It further stressed that "censorship of books . . . must be challenged by libraries in maintenance of their responsibility to provide public information and enlightenment through the printed word."

So the library in San Antonio had fought for and won its freedom from the self-appointed censors, yet damage had been done. The Minute Women's list received wide circulation among like organizations and other volunteer censors in many other localities.

Librarians continued through the decade of the fifties to press for the freedom to read, and in this they were greatly aided by President Dwight D. Eisenhower's letter to their annual conference. "Our librarians," the President wrote, "serve the precious liberties of our nation: freedom of inquiry, freedom of the spoken and written word, freedom of exchange of ideas. . . .

"But we know that freedom cannot be served by the devices of the tyrant. As it is an ancient truth that freedom cannot be legislated into existence, so it is no less obvious that freedom cannot be censored into existence. And any who act as if freedom's defenses are to be found in suppression and suspicion and fear confess a doctrine that is alien to America. . . ."

For many many years individuals and groups have used pressure in censorship attempts. To be sure, most would deny that their efforts were directed toward censorship, but rather toward maintaining community standards and protecting the youth.

In Rockledge, Florida, near Cape Kennedy, the city council in 1970 acted to keep *Playboy* magazine under the counter. *Playboy*, a monthly, often contains pictures of nudes, although its publisher states that it is "not obscene. No issue of the magazine has ever been ruled obscene." Yet one of Rockledge's councilmen had received complaints that the magazine was displayed near where children purchased candy. He took these complaints to the city council meeting, the matter was discussed and all agreed that candy and *Playboy* did not mix.

The possibility of having the publication removed from magazine racks at the town's convenience stores was discussed, but the city attorney advised that the best way to achieve that goal would be to talk the matter over with the store managers. The mayor of the city and four or five councilmen visited various stores and "everyone was in agreement to sell the magazine from under the counter." The mayor commented that putting *Playboy* under the counter would still "give decent exposure to indecent exposure." He went on to say that the "people of Rockledge are objecting to sale of this type of material and we want what is best for the city. It was on a strictly voluntary basis."

Private pressure was again successful. Self-judgments were made and imposed on all. And that has always been where the danger lay.

CHAPTER 12

The Only Sure Weapon

FROM THE beginning of recorded history until the present day there has been cultural censorship of one form or another. Through the years no medium of communication has been totally free. The bookseller of The Hierophant in Annapolis in 1969 was a victim of censorship (and entrapment) as were hundreds of booksellers, publishers, and authors in the past. Magazines, movies, plays, art, have all felt the brush of the censor.

The courts, as we have seen, have for years been called upon to act as the supreme and final censors in the United States. It is interesting to note that the early years of our country were free from attempts to impose cultural censorship; it was only a little over 150 years ago that the first such case in the United States came to the attention of the courts. Since that time the clamor of the censors has increased, case after case has been tried, precedents of law have been established. And as we have seen, as the courts became more and more liberal in their interpretations, and freedoms in the arts burst forth into flower with less and less inhibitions, the pressures from self-appointed censors grew.

Yet one must have a sense of and knowledge of history before raising a cry of alarm about the permissiveness of our present society and the need to control it by repression of the arts. Each society has its own standards. The old Roman Empire was corrupt and it fell as a result of its own excesses, not because of repression. If our society becomes corrupt, it becomes corrupt because we, its citizens, become corrupt. If we are subverted, it is because we allow ourselves to become subverted. The most priceless heritage we have is our freedom and if censors close the doors to our freedom by dictating what we may read, see, or hear, then we face the greatest danger.

The clamor for repression has been concentrated on what is called obscene, and that seems to have a direct relationship to sex. The obscene will be censored, yet what will come next? In an area of such subjective judgment, who can tell? Will an objection to a political or religious viewpoint be cause for censorship? (It has been; remember all the books removed from libraries because of their subversive nature.) Where do the rights of the censor begin, and where do they end?

Great men in this country have had serious thoughts on the question. Perhaps Thomas Jefferson spoke most eloquently for the freedom of the people in his country.

In 1813, a Frenchman named Regnault de Bécourt called to Jefferson's attention a book he had written entitled *Sur la Création du Monde, ou Système d'Organisation Primitive,* for he knew of Jefferson's wide interest in past and present literature. Jefferson thought that this book on the creation of the world might be worthwhile so he authorized his usual book dealer in Philadelphia to pay $2 to the French author for the work. Jefferson was disappointed in the book when he received it, for it seemed to be just a simple attack on Sir Isaac Newton's system of philosophy. However, much more was to occur. The bookshop owner was visited by the Philadelphia police and taken to court on the charge of vending subversive if not blasphemous literature. Jefferson was notified, and cleared up the matter that it was he who had ordered the book and the bookseller was merely an agent in the transaction. The police were quieted, but Jefferson was aroused to an impassioned statement which reflected his whole philosophy. Earlier he had declared: "I have sworn upon the altar of God eternal hostility against every form of tyranny over the mind of man." Now he was to write to the bookseller:

"I really am mortified to be told that, in the *United States of America,* a fact like this can become a subject of inquiry, and of criminal inquiry too, as an offense against religion: that a question about the sale of a book can be carried before the civil magistrate. Is this then our freedom of religion? And are we to have a censor whose imprimatur shall say what books may be sold, and what we may buy? And who is thus to dogmatize religious opinions for our citizens? Whose foot is to be the measure to which ours are all to be cut or stretched? Is a priest to be our inquisitor? Or shall a layman, simple as ourselves, set up his reason as the rule for what we are to read, and what we must believe?

"It is an insult to our citizens to question whether they are rational beings or not; and blasphemy against religion to suppose it cannot stand a test of truth and reason . . . let us hear both sides, if we choose."

Another great leader, from another time, Whitney Griswold, President of Yale, said: "Books won't stay banned. They won't burn. Ideas won't go to jail. In the long run of history, the censor and the inquisitor have always lost. The only sure weapon against bad ideas is better ideas."

Perhaps the reader will agree that free men cannot remain free if their eyes, ears, and minds are fettered. That is the whole point of this book.

Bibliography

Books

Boyer, Paul S., *Purity in Print: The Vice-Society Movement and Book Censorship in America.* New York: Charles Scribner's Sons, 1968.

Broun, Heywood, and Leech, Margaret, *Anthony Comstock, Roundsman of the Lord.* New York: Albert and Charles Boni, 1927.

Clor, Harry M., *Obscenity and Public Morality.* Chicago: University of Chicago Press, 1969.

Downs, Robert, ed., *The First Freedom.* Chicago: American Library Association, 1960.

Ernst, Morris L., and Schwartz, Alan U., *Censorship: The Search for the Obscene.* New York: Macmillan Co., 1964.

Gardiner, Harold C., *Catholic Viewpoint on Censorship.* Garden City, New York: Charles Scribner's Sons, 1968.

Perrin, Noel, *Dr. Bowdler's Legacy.* New York: Atheneum, 1969.

Rucker, Bryce W., *The First Freedom.* Carbondale, Illinois: Southern Illinois University Press, 1968.

Additional Sources

Crowther, Bosley, *Movies and Censorship*, Public Affairs Pamphlet No. 332. New York: Public Affairs Committee, 1962.

Johnson, Nicholas, "What Do We Do About Television?" *Saturday Review*, July 11, 1970, p. 14.

Motion Picture Association of America, New York City: *How the Public Has Accepted the Motion Picture Industry's New Code and Rating Program; It's the Treatment That Counts; A Landmark Decision in Motion Picture Censorship; The Motion Picture Code and Rating Program; The Motion Picture Code of Self-Regulation; The Motion Picture Production Code; Movies and Self-Regulation; Which Films are OK for Our Children* (a reprint from *Together* magazine, February, 1969).

National Association of Broadcasters, Washington, D.C.: *Free Television: How It Serves America; History of the National Association of Broadcasters; The Radio Code; Radio, U.S.A.; Study Guide on Broadcasting; The Television Code.*

New York Society for the Suppression of Vice, New York City: Annual Reports, 1874 to present.

Scott, Barbara, "Censorship and/or Classification." *The Journal of the Producers Guild of America*, December, 1968.

Index